Frederick the Great and the United States of America

With a supplement:
The United States and Maritime Law

Friedrich Kapp

1871

Translated & Compiled by Joshua Lutz

Published in Louisville, KY

Paperback ISBN 978-1-7363352-0-8
Ebook ISBN 978-1-7363352-1-5
Library of Congress Control Number: 2020925197

Eltville Publishing LLC
contact@eltvillepublishing.com

Translator's Note:

In translating this work, I have tried to alter Mr. Kapp's words as little as possible. I have adjusted them where a more contemporary style would benefit the reader but have stuck to the original terms and spelling more often than not. Of the quotes contained in the book, I have reverted some of them back to the original 18th-century English versions. I also took the responsibility of inserting footnotes where I considered it beneficial. It is my hope that these slight changes and additions will render an enhanced experience of this fantastic and informative historical work for the reader.

—Joshua Lutz

Contents

Foreword

The present work concludes the task which I undertook during a twenty-year sojourn in the United States.

This task attempts to prove the influence that Germany exerted on the development of the American republic and to recount the participation it had in the nation's history, according to the sources. After my previous work, in which the positions of people, generals, and soldiers regarding events were written about; my research regarding the exposition of Frederick the Great's relationship to the United States still remained to be concluded.

What I discovered through American sources, I released at the end of 1864 in the "Deutsche Jahrbücher" monthly journal of H. B. Oppenheim. In its current revision, my presentation has been enriched and completed thanks to the handwritten riches of the confidential state archives. The subject at hand has gained a heightened interest due in part due to its relation to the present day. Therefore, I believe the appendix, which follows for strictly historical purposes, does not require any special justification.

Of my printed sources, I consider the Diplomatic Correspondence of the United States of America from 1776-1783, Volume

12, Washington 1833, and the Diplomatic Correspondence from 1783-1789, Volume 3, Washington 1837 to be the most important. Additionally, the biographies and collective works of Franklin, John Adams, Jefferson, Washington, and Arthur Lee.

I do not know whether or not the Washington state archives still possess papers about the defined time period, which they did not release to me, but I find that hard to believe. In my experiences there, I am compelled to point out that I was never refused, under false pretext, by any officials.

On the contrary, I cannot acknowledge the generosity enough with which I was allowed to use the confidential state archives and the friendly support which I found there. Above all, I extend the utmost thanks to the archive advisers, Mr. Friedländer and Mr. von Moerner, for the assistance they have given me in such rich abundance.

I am especially indebted to Mr. George Bancroft for the numerous transcripts from the English archives, which were most kindly shared with me. These are denoted as St. P. O. (State Paper Office) where cited.

The style of writing of the king and the untranslated documents are kept unchanged.

Berlin, February 22, 1871.

Friedrich Kapp.

Frederick the Great and the United States of America

In the already extensive library of literature about Frederick the Great, the position of the king to the American War of Independence and his later dealings with the United States are only discussed incidentally or not at all. These dealings certainly occupy an inferior rank in his foreign politics. The reasons for that are obvious. At one time, the interests of Prussia and those of the distant continent touched very little. At that time, the already aging Frederick was much more engaged with nearer laying plans rather than in an intervention in the American war or a rash approach to the young transatlantic republic. Overall, it seemed advisable to give attention to newer, far better-looking political missions. Shortly before the outbreak of the American Revolution, the securing of acquired possessions by the First Partition of Poland – the Russian-Oriental politics – and the conflict of the War of the Bavarian Succession – the German politics – demanded all available forces and the undivided attention of the king. Nevertheless, evaluation and disapproval of the English politics are exposed in his meager relationship to the United States, as well as a remarkable solicitude for the Prussian commercial interests and the connection between the aspired goals and the means set in motion to achieve them. On the other hand, these dealings have been distorted in such a politically biased fashion by celebrated historians that Frederick's position regarding the United States deserves to be the subject of an independent examination.

This task is divided into two complementary parts: the first outlines the king's relationship to the revolution, and the second, the saga of the completion of the Prussian-American Treaty of Amity and Commerce during the international law era.

Frederick's Attitude towards the Revolution

Regarding the subject at hand, there are two motives to distinguish in the king's politics. First is the endeavor to increase the Prussian commercial industry and, above all, to expand the East Frisian maritime trade through the development of the American markets. The second, his bitterness against England and the desire to inflict loss on England when possible, but only where it would not harm Prussian interests.

The hate of Frederick towards England had its natural and justifiable reasons. From the first days of his accession to the throne, his uncle, George II, stood against him and spared no means to oppress the young, aspiring king and decrease his power. Hannover was the central point of the continental politics of both George I and George II.[1] In their eyes, their Electorate lost influence and standing if Prussia elevated itself and continued to rise, rather than if Prussia were undermined and humiliated. Instead

1 When Queen Anne died in 1714, the throne passed to her closest Protestant relative due to Catholics being barred from ruling. This fell to her German second cousin, George I, and began the Hanoverian dynasty of British Monarchs who still retained their possessions in Germany.

of being determined and guided by large-scale points of view by intervening in European politics, George II only knew the interests of his home country and even sacrificed the power position of England. So, at the outbreak of the War of the Austrian Succession, he aligned himself with Maria Theresia out of fear of losing Hannover. This resulted in Frederick being forced to the side of France. The taking possession and claiming of East Frisia by the King of Prussia only enlarged the already established irritability between both rulers. Even when England stepped back from the confederation that stood against Frederick in the summer of 1745 during the second War of the Austrian Succession and later mediated the peace with the Queen, it would still not alleviate the personal mistrust of both kings against one another. Even after the Treaty of Aachen, George thought to entice the Prussian ruler, who had already reached European significance, with subsidies. Moreover, to put him in his place next to the king of Sardinia.[2]

In 1749, the English cabinet wanted to elect Archduke Joseph as Holy Roman Emperor to hold Prussia's ambition in check. Between 1748 and 1756, England advanced the tension of both courts through their reckless action at sea and on land. During this whole time, both nations only retained representatives who they themselves certified. George was only compelled to approach his nephew again after the cooling off of the relationship between England and the Vienna court, and because of the looming Seven Years War. Hoping to protect Hannover against the great European coalition through Frederick, he concluded the Treaty of Westminster with Prussia in 1756 and was pressed to rush aid to Prussia in its war efforts soon thereafter. Playing his double

2 Sardinia received financial and naval support from England to fight battles in this war, yet at the treaty negotiations, was relegated to an inferior status and gained little.

game, George tried to induce a peace with the Empress Maria Theresia while assuring Frederick of his unwavering allegiance and friendship.

Only with Pitt's second entry in office did English politics appear to again be dominated from a higher nationalistic standpoint. Pitt tried to defend England's American colonies against the French through Frederick in Germany. In 1758, he expanded the previous neutrality agreement into the Anglo-Prussian Convention. In doing so, truly not to his fatherland's damage, he fortified loyalty to the valiant ally during the last year of George II's reign. But George III's ascension to the throne and the nomination of John Stuart, 3rd Earl of Bute as foreign minister (October 1761), changed these favorable relations for both sides in one fell swoop. Seldom has an ally been more disgracefully abandoned, indeed betrayed, than Frederick was by Minister Bute. Frederick was denied the subsidies for 1762 when he needed them most. Additionally, to win the friendship of Maria Theresia against France, the province of Silesia, which was a possession of the former ally and the initial subject of dispute during the war in Germany, was offered as compensation. Not satisfied with this, Peter III[3] sought to discourage this out of his admiration for Frederick and offered 100,000 pounds as a bribe for the attainment of this object of the Kaiser's domain. Peter informed Frederick, the friend he so admired, about this most disdainful offer to win Prussia over with the Prussian province of Silesia. The petty aristocratic English cabinet viewed the Prussian king as a third-tier prince that they could push to the side, or as a poor stipend holder they could mistreat with impunity. But they would soon recognize that they had miscalculated Frederick. In the most challenging time of the war, when

3 Peter III of Russia, German-born who barely spoke Russian and was very pro-Prussian.

the outlook on his downfall outweighed the hope of an eventual success tenfold, that same proud and confident man wrote in a famous letter to Pitt that he only governed by two principles. By honor, which forbids him to sacrifice an inch of land, and by the interest of his country, which compels him to spill the last drops of blood for the glory and the welfare of his people. This unshakable character did not allow him to dictate terms to his allies. As Bute restricted the granting of further subsidies, wanting to make them contingent upon ridiculous stipulations, Frederick shouted with outrage, "This Englishman imagines that money can do everything and that it is only found in England!" He then led the war to a triumphant end without Bute's aid.

Even after the Treaty of Paris, the provisions of which were drafted at times intentionally harmful to Prussia[4] and hence poured new oil on the flames, England persisted with its hate against Frederick. Up until the outbreak of the American Revolution, they missed no opportunity to display it. Under Pitt, it was understood that the liberal evolution of Europe was at stake if Russia, France, and Austria were united; therefore, their own interests rested on Prussia. Bute and his successor engaged themselves in the impossible task of winning over Russia and Austria, isolating France, and completely excluding Prussia from the "Concert of Europe."[5] After the Seven Years War, it was absurd to act as if Frederick the Great did not even exist. As a result of England pushing Frederick in other directions, particularly into Russia's arms, it had directed European politics on an unnatural course for

4 Considered a British betrayal, Prussia was not considered in this treaty that settled the Seven Years War. Thus, Prussia was forced to negotiate separately.

5 Refers to the diplomacy among the great powers of the time to avoid conflicts, both internal and external, and maintain the status quo.

almost a full century, thereby establishing Russia's influence and predominance without increasing England's importance.

England celebrated just one single, insignificant triumph over Frederick during the whole decade following the Seven Years War. As it was not likely to undermine his alliance with Catherine II, England finally succeeded in persuading the Russian empress to oppose the Prussian claim on the possession of Gdansk at the first Partition of Poland and thereby thwarted one of the dearest wishes of the king. Russian and English jealousies coincided here in their animosity against the power increase and commerce of Prussia. Otherwise, England, who at that time exerted neither weight nor influence on the affairs of the continent, would have hardly penetrated in this case as well. This bitterness that went back decades explained Frederick's position to England at the outbreak of the American Revolutionary War.

Alongside their hatred, the English diplomats had a secret fear of Frederick's mental superiority and diplomatic craftiness. He was held responsible for almost every disappointment that their politics met. Sir J. Harris, the later Lord Malmesbury, wrote to Frederick on 9. Dec 1775, with utterly unfounded blame over the failed English attempt to acquisition a Russian auxiliary corps. In another letter, he suggested that the style and manner in which his Prussian Majesty conducted business was so mysterious that he constantly deceived the watchfulness and inquiries of even the most experienced people in order to conceal his political plans. Suffolk feared from the beginning that Frederick would avenge the most sensitive insults by transferring Prussian officers to the Americans. In short, at the outbreak of the war, all English ministers and diplomats had an evil moral sense and, therefore, great fear of Frederick's vengeance. At that time, no officers were sent to train the warfare-inexperienced Separatists in America because he wasn't approached by anyone. In the beginning, he assumed, and intentionally feigned, only an amicable concern in their results.

Contrary to the Americans, England did not have a single friend or ally due to its petty and clumsy politics. Rather, they had only enemies, both open and secret. "All of Europe," would Franklin justly write home on April 9, 1777, "wishes England to be humiliated, as it has offended all nations through its show of arrogance at every opportunity during times of fortune."

Benjamin Franklin's "Edict of the King of Prussia,"[6] in which the famous Quaker mocked the unreasonable treatment of the colonies by the motherland, proclaimed that since the existing England was founded by Hengist and Horsa and other German chieftains, the Prussian king had the legal claim to collect taxes in England, to forbid exports and send criminals from Prussia to England. This so-called edict was dated and notarized as legitimate by a secretary on August 25, 1773, in Potsdam. Franklin wrote to his son William on October 6, 1773, "I was down at Lord de Spencer's when the post brought that day's paper. Mr. Paul Whitehead was there too, who runs early through all the papers, and tells the company what he finds remarkable. He had them in another room, and we were chatting in the breakfast parlour when he came running in to us, out of breath, with the paper in his hand. 'Here!' says he, 'here's news for ye! Here's the king of Prussia, claiming a right to this kingdom!' Everyone stared at him, I as much as anybody. As Whitehead read two or three sentences, one of the people present cried out, 'Damn his impudence!

6 One of Benjamin Franklin's famous satires, in which he writes as the King of Prussia, suggesting Britain be ruled under the same rationale Britain uses to justify its rule of the American colonies.

I dare say we will hear by next post that he is upon his march with 100,000 men to support his claim.' But Whitehead, on further reading, soon noticed the fun and said 'I'll be hanged if this is not one of your Yankee jokes upon us.'"[7]

The English Tories so hated Frederick, the opposition was so suspicious of him. Yet he was so popular with the people of the motherland and, at the same time, there was no more popular ruler in the American colonies than the king of Prussia. In the interests of European warfare, the English had considered him, after Pitt, as the hero of Protestantism (!) and as the champion of their beliefs against the papacy and the sinister powers of the Middle Ages. The Puritans of New England prayed in unison with the citizens of old England for the success of his weapons and celebrated the victories of the atheistic king as national successes. "Because his victories," said Jonathan Mayhew[8] of Boston, "are our own." In the middle states, particularly New York and Pennsylvania, the admiration for the king was no less prevalent. Themselves the offspring of immigrated Germans, they felt elevated through him and celebrated his victories, especially the Battle of Rossbach,[9] which was such a humiliation to those haughty French who had driven their parents and grandparents on the Rhine and in Swabia out of house and home in the past. Still today, in central Pennsylvania and even in Philadelphia taverns, toasts of "to the king of Prussia" can be heard. Frederick can often be found on both weathered and newly-painted signs above the entrances and the dusted and yellowed old pictures in the rooms – in the same historic uniform

---

7 The Works of Benjamin Franklin, VIII, 89-91.

8 Famous minister known for his sermons championing colonial liberties.

9 Decisive battle against a much larger force, considered one of Frederick's most outstanding strategic achievements.

with his three-cornered hat and cane, the same way he is admired in the villages of his homeland.

Privately, the leading minds of the American Revolution also regarded the king as one of their own and had revered him as an ally and hero of the Protestant faith since their early days. He was viewed as the arbitrator and wisest man of Europe in their eyes and as the ruler who must stand on their side due to his intellectual superiority and the supposed equivalence of his goals to theirs. Contemporary speeches and pamphlets even compared the oppression of the young republic with the embarrassments of the king in the Seven Years War. They urged the listener and reader to channel the courage to endure and follow through with the fight from his fortitude and bravery. Every statement of the king against England, every measure against the soul-selling German princes, was actively spread and exaggerated during the war with particular bias. In a letter to Lafayette, Washington called it the highest possible honor to be received by such a great statesman and general as Frederick. Franklin even fabricated anecdotes to either anger the English or to display the king's sympathy for the fighting colonies: like his alleged remark that the livestock tax should be levied on those Hessians passing through Minden.

Greene, the most significant general of the revolution after Washington, once glorified himself in a letter to Steuben by stating that he had so cleverly created and executed a maneuver that it would have even secured Frederick's approval. Steuben found such inclined ears for his reforms from the beginning because, since he had been an aide-de-camp and student of the king, he understood his affairs more thoroughly than anybody else. In the mid-1780s, Jefferson said in a letter he wrote back home that Frederick's forthcoming death was a world history event and European tragedy.

Even today in America, it is commonly thought that Frederick expressed his recognition of Washington by sending him a sword of honor. Even academic periodicals repeated this believable fable, based on the fact that the Prussian gunsmith, Theophilus Alte, gifted Washington a beautiful hand-made saber with an admiring inscription.

Incidentally, the king has received honorable and righteous acknowledgement in the American historiography in his deliberate opposition to England in the present day. Compare Bancroft's masterful portrayal of Frederick, which testifies to the comprehension of the king and his time in every word, with the shallow caricature by Macaulay, which is nothing more than a lampoon of the author on himself and in which the historiography is degraded through scandal and gossip.

Of course, Frederick sought to exploit England's war with its colonies for his own interests whenever possible. In particular, he expected to gain great advantages for the commerce of East Frisia from the war. This province, about 54 square miles in size with around 100,000 inhabitants, had only been in Prussian possession since 1744. Since then, its commerce had cultivated special attention from the king. Through its location on the North Sea and some not insignificant harbors, it was fitting for Prussia to secure at least a modest share of the world trade. At the same time, Frederick's efforts were continuously aimed at expanding the commerce of the other provinces, especially the sale of Silesian linen, through the elevation of East Frisia and also obtaining cheap tobacco from America. He had elevated Emden to a free port in 1751, in 1750, founded there an Asiatic, and in 1753, a Bengali trading company for the German export and import trade. Maritime mayflies, who, of course, were swept away without a trace at the first political storm in the Seven Years War, are only noteworthy experiments which certainly testify more to the good intentions of the king than to his insight of the indispensable conditions of maritime trade.

The merchants of Emden, Leer, and Norden tried to continue to operate on this course after the breakdown of these high-flying plans. They even sent ships to China, the East Indies, and America; and reached the height of their luster at the outbreak of the American war, when the Dutch and some of Bremen's merchants flew the neutral Prussian flag for their freights. Frederick was convinced that genuine relations would arise again with the return of peace, so this unexpected upturn of the East Frisian commerce was very welcome. On the advice of his Minister of Commerce, Schulenburg, who believed he had found a hitherto neglected source of inexhaustible wealth through the encouragement of herring fishing, the king exerted everything to pull at least some of the commerce from Amsterdam to Emden and elevate the port to a great world market. This plan seemed practicable because, due to the breakaway of the colonies from England, which so far had monopolized the trade to America, they were now opened up to competition from the other European nations and because Prussia had already exported various articles via England to America, such as fabric and ironware.

Silas Deane,[10] known as the first agent that Congress sent to Paris for the establishment of diplomatic and commercial contacts, had barely arrived in the summer of 1776 before he was in contact with the Prussian commercial agent, Monttessuy,

10 The first U.S. foreign diplomat, Deane was integral in securing French aid and enlisting foreign military personnel but was later accused of embezzlement and being a traitor.

and asked him if he could obtain weapons and munitions from Prussia for the United States. Monttessuy, a Berliner from one of the French colonies, had served for Frederick in Paris since 1771. He was active and agile but a bit too eager and fiery. The Prussian trade minister Schulenburg said that he was a very useful man that one must hold close so he does not overstep his instructions. Without inquiring about the means for the possible execution of such a request, he had nothing more urgent to do on July 29, 1776, than to notify the king of the request from Deane and propose an American-Prussian trade agreement to him.

"Where the trade with America is concerned," he wrote on August 9, 1776, to Schulenburg, "it is a bit too hazardous, for it would be a great loss if the ships were to be taken. But if he wants to supply Virginian tobacco leaves to my tobacco administration on very favorable terms and not so expensive as before, that is something more likely to be done. I, therefore, want to instruct you to coordinate closely with my private financial counsel, Magusch, over the price of the Virginian tobacco."

The royal tobacco administration expended 2,000 barrels of American tobacco annually at that time. But as a result of the unrest in the colonies, it became more expensive with each day, and in 1776 it was barely available anymore in English and French ports. In 1773, the cost per pound in London was: brown long-leaved Virginia 2 1/8 d., yellow Marylander 2 7/8 d., medium Swiccut 2 3/16, best Swiccut 2 9/16 d., fine Lux 2 7/8 d., fine yellow Maryland 3d. and York River Swiccut likewise, at 3 d. Sterling.[11]

Schulenburg forwarded to Monttessuy the following posed questions from the private financial counsel Magusch for the American agents to answer on September 12, 1776. Included was the notice upfront that they could not admit a sale of weapons and

11 d.; abbreviation for pence in British currency.

munitions to America but would gladly undertake an exchange of other products:

1. Whether the tobacco plantations will continue unabated, even those which the ownership to English households is entitled? Whether there are still great stocks in the colonies, and if much has already been exported to other European harbors, and to which?

2. Whether American households or seafarers want to assume deliveries of tobacco, at what price, and to which harbors? For example, Cadiz or a Dutch or Danish location in the West Indies such as Sint Eustatius? Is it possible to consider Emden?

3. Whether the colonies insist that they want to barter war munitions in exchange, or if they seek other local products like linen, ironware, woolen wares, or if cash payment at the place of delivery is desired?

Deane answered these questions generally that the stated tobacco varieties out of Virginia and Maryland could be obtained directly and that payment would gladly be accepted in linen, woolen fabrics, copper, lead, and steel. He also noted specifically:

1. The colonies cultivate tobacco as they always have. A quantity is immediately available which can be shipped, with a small shipment in European and in Scottish hands.

2. At this time, supplying tobacco to a person living in Paris must be done under one of the following conditions: at the American cost price of four Sous Tournois (25% less valuable than Parisian currency) per pound, 5% commission, freight and insurance; or at the Dutch or French market price at

the time of the arrival in Europe if one wants to undertake the risk himself. The port of delivery may be Sint Eustatius, St Croix and St Thomas in America, or Amsterdam and Emden in Europe.

3. Weapons and munitions or the mentioned goods can serve as payment; the designated person commits to delivery of 2,000 barrels or more. The market price in America is only two deniers sterling per pound; however, the risk is very significant due to the war.

"Do not forget Prussia," wrote Deane on October 1, 1776, to the committee of secret correspondence, "it is of the greatest importance that someone be employed who will parley with the king. I am familiar with his local agents and even prepared an answer on various questions and proposals which he has presented to me about the American trade. France and Spain are our natural allies, while the Italian states need our grain and some other goods. Prussia, always thinking to promote its own interests, needs only inquiries about those facts that affect the daily increasing of trade with America, which does benefit us too."[12]

At the same time, Monttessuy saw cause, on his own accountability, to explain to Deane that the king would like it if an American came to Berlin and would give detailed information verbally about the benefits of the attached goods in America.[13] Deane thought that they should not miss this advantageous opportunity for a ruler to take an interest in American independence, one who has tried to make Emden into a second Amsterdam for

12 The Diplomatic Correspondence of the American Revolution, Vol. I, 45.

13 The Diplomatic Correspondence of the American Revolution, Vol. IX, 346.

years. William Carmichael, a young Marylander who had earlier volunteered as secretary to Deane, was prompted to travel to Berlin. Schulenburg was nothing less than delighted with the arbitrary actions of his agents. On October 21, 1776, he questioned the king over the rules of conduct at Carmichael's arrival in Berlin. Whether he should undertake further on the matter with Carmichael, and how he should be received. The king personally wrote this advice in passing: "Receive him well, but it will not last long because the English have beaten the colonies."

"This insurgent," as Monttessuy called the young Carmichael in his letter of introduction, was happy to show his eagerness for the glorious cause which concerned politics and humanity in the same manner and therefore was given so much importance in the eyes of Europe. He went in the autumn of 1776 via Amsterdam to Berlin. He arrived there on November 21 and applied for an audience with Schulenburg on the 22nd, who politely but reluctantly received him. Carmichael showed himself to be well-educated about the affairs of his fatherland in the subsequent meetings and won the favor of the minister just as much through his valuable information about American products and his praise of Prussian products as through his humble yet determined demeanor. The establishment of trade relations only posed great difficulty because the Americans could not send ships to Dutch or German ports due to the impossibility of insuring their cargo. Not wanting to run such great risk, Prussia at last composed a plan to land the tobacco in Brittany and re-export it from there to Germany, thus breaking the monopoly of the French general leaseholders.

On December 2, 1776, the king replied to Schulenburg's report: "As favorable as the proposals and trade plans of Mr. Carmichael may appear, we must not rush anything with him. To fulfill them through a formal trade agreement is a thing of impossibility, and likewise, an opening of direct trade with his homeland is a matter that presents a thousand difficulties. If his countrymen want to land the Virginian tobacco in a Brittany harbor at their own risk, so am I therewith agreed, and I will instruct the Baron Goltz in Paris to secretly support all steps, which this agent will do, to obtain the permits for the re-exportation of this tobacco to my states."

But one such permit was not received, and the king did not want to run the risk in the present for possible benefits in the future, so the negotiations were broken off. However, Carmichael remained in correspondence with Schulenburg and still wrote to him, even in 1780 from Madrid, where he had gone as Secretary to the Legation. The Prussian minister treated him the same as before, with great regard and friendly kindness. The American negotiator left Berlin on December 6, 1776, after, last but not least, he had excited the attention of the English legation. "Approximately 3 weeks ago," the English legation secretary, Barnier, wrote on December 14, 1776, from Berlin to home, "a young man of very fine exterior named Carmichael arrived here from Paris via Hamburg who, as I have reason to suspect, is a rebel emissary. During the 8 or 10 days of his local stay, he had frequent meetings with the Prussian minister, as it seems to me, to make proposals on the establishment of trade relations with the insurgent provinces. At least so I've heard from people, with whom he made the highest pressing to the price and quality of the rough cloth fabricated here. Perhaps he may have also suggested to send some Prussian officers to America to drill the rebel army. He left Berlin on Thursday, 8 days ago, and went via Leipzig and Dresden back to Paris, but meanwhile intends to return here soon."

Count Finckenstein,[14] one of the Prussian foreign ministers, explained to the English envoy on his polite official query that there was no truth to the rumors of the reception of a rebel agent. Carmichael came to Berlin as a private individual and was only received by the Minister of Commerce and that the king maintained too great a friendship for England to enter into any sort of connections with rebellious subjects.

Carmichael had barely returned to Paris when Benjamin Franklin, Silas Deane, and Arthur Lee were appointed official commissioners to Europe on September 26, 1776. The first two mentioned that the negotiations with Schulenburg had resumed and wrote from Paris on February 14, 1777, as follows:

"We have the honor of enclosing to your Excellency the Declaration of the Independency of the United States of North America, with the Articles of their Confederation, which we desire you to take the earliest Opportunity of laying before His Majesty, the King of Prussia. At the same time, we wish he may be assured of the earnest desire of the United States to obtain his friendship; and by a free commerce to establish an intercourse between their distant countries, which they are confident must be mutually beneficial. We shall, if agreeable to His Majesty, lay before him the state of the commerce of the United States and the advantages which must result to both countries from the establishment of a commercial intercourse. In the meantime we take the liberty of assuring your Excellency that the reports of the advantages gained by his Britannic Majesty's Troops over those of the United States are greatly exaggerated, and many of them without foundation, especially those which assert that an accommodation is about to

14 Karl Wilhelm Finck von Finckenstein was the leading force in Prussia's foreign affairs. He was even declared Regent of Prussia by Frederick in the event of his death or capture.

take place, there being no probability of such an Event by the latest intelligence we have received from America."

The timing for such proposals could not have been more inconvenient. The whole world was still under the impression of the defeats that the American troops had suffered from the end of August until the end of November 1776 in New York and New Jersey, whereas the successes won by Washington at Trenton and Princeton still had not reached Europe. Nevertheless, Frederick carefully considered the revelations made to him, and on March 12, 1777, issued the following cabinet order to Schulenburg, which follows unabridged because it completely articulates outright the reasons for his existing and future policies for the warring colonies.

"I sense, as well as you do," said the king, "all of the obstacles which stand in the way of direct trade with the English possessions in America. Since I am without a navy and have neither a fleet nor armed ships for its protection, we must carry out this trade under a foreign flag. As such we have only the Dutch, who incidentally now gets just as little respect from England as the others. However, in spite these considerations, I do not wish to offend the colonies through a complete rejection of the propositions of their commissioners in Paris. Therefore, it seems to me most appropriate that you attempt to maintain a good atmosphere. In this respect, you can let them know the following: I would gladly establish this trade relationship, but the above-mentioned obstacles do not allow to send goods to the Americans in my own ships. Even if I operate under a foreign flag, it would always be at risk before the English surveillance squadron. There is no American port known to me where these ships can unload. Even Sint Eustatius offers no safe haven because there are English ships in its vicinity, which would never let through this shipment of goods. For this reason, I expect further explanation from the agents about the ways and means with which such trade can be put in progress at this time. This way the mentioned colonies will not feel offended, and we will always be in the position to negotiate with them, as soon as perhaps the economic situation becomes more favorable. Then our Silesian linen, fabric and other goods can find a new market there. Since the banker Schütz has more understanding than you and I of such trade, you would do well to hear his views in order to take advantage of it and to make use of it when we issue a response to the American agents. As for the goods to be exported as return freight, the Virginian tobacco seems to me a staple which easily would bring 200,000 Thalers. So, I recommend you do not include anything in your response to the agents that could harm or insult their employers. Instead talk about their offer as favorable as possible so that we can immediately exploit this when the circumstances arise."

Based on these instructions, Schulenburg replied to the American agents on March 15, 1777, and achieved the resumption of the discussions. The Americans now went a step further. First, they asked the king to prevent the leasing of further German troops against their country. Then they offered to give oral reports about the commerce and the resources of America through Arthur Lee, one of their own who had arrived in Paris in the meantime. This mission appeared especially urgent and important to them because, above all, they must have a port in the North Sea for the arrival and the outfitting of their privateers as well as for the sale of their prizes. It was not difficult to conceal such equipage under all possible excuses and, at worst, to prevent discovery through a timely warning. This proved to be a greater difficulty at the prize sale since this, of course, was public. As accommodating as France was otherwise to the Americans, such as with well-known financial support, when the American Captain Cunningham brought the English ship "Prince of Orange" as prize to Dunkerque, they would not release it without due process by the British government. Instead, they arrested the captain and immediately sent his accomplices to the Bastille.[15] If one wanted to seriously disrupt and jeopardize the northern trade of the English, one must have a North Sea port. Prussia, as the holder of Frisia, was the sole power that could grant one for such use, as the Dutch wouldn't dare to excite the displeasure of England. Thus, it was the commissioner's chief concern to obtain this permission from the king. The expectation was that it was too risky, with just the intention to elevate Emden, to recognize the Americans and let a war with England come. In any case, the matter seemed worth an attempt to them. For if the whole objective was not reached, they could still perhaps secure other advantages.

"We have the commands from the Congress of the United States"- wrote Franklin, Deane, and Lee from Paris on April 19, 1777, to Schulenburg, "to inform His Prussian majesty's ambassadors here that our government intends to send a minister to Berlin as soon as possible who is proper authorized to discuss over various important affairs. We are also instructed by Congress to solicit the friendship of your court and to request that it afford no aid to our enemies, but to help prevent the landing of hired troops sent for our annihilation where possible. Lastly, to offer free trade with the United States for Prussian nationals. One of us will hurry to attend your Excellency, to verbally detail the circumstances and resources of America, the importance of its trade and

15 The Diplomatic Correspondence of the American Revolution, Vol. I, 292-293.

the ways on which it can be operated to mutual advantage. With the great importance which free trade has for both countries, we hope to overcome the difficulties mentioned in your excellency's letter from March 15th, and are convinced that a great share of the American trade can be directed to Prussia without risk or great expense."

Schulenburg requested instructions from the king on 5 May 1777, regarding these new proposals, translations enclosed, from the American agents, who answered on May 6 as follows:

"I was already informed by Baron Goltz in Paris of the intention of the English colonies in America that they wanted to have an authorized minister at my court, and likewise of the letter that their agents sent to you. I thank you for the translation, which you have submitted to me at the end of your reports, but it seems to me as though the colonies are a little too hasty in their proposals by already making them the subject of a formal negotiation. Their affairs are still in great crisis and still lack very much the solid foundation that their independence is to be built on. The success of their weapons can alone determine, and this changes with every moment. In fact, it seems the immediate opening of trade with them under the current economic situation exposes unlimited risks because 80 to 90 English ships which swarm about on several seas would take everything from us. It is so true that a power that has no navy can't count on their merchant flags to be respected in wartime. That is why our merchant ships hitherto travel no further than Russia and Cadiz, and that they still have not appeared in more distant waters where their trade would run greater risks. As long as the independence of the colonies is not more strongly fortified than at this time, every direct trade guided under my flag seems to me too dangerous and subject to too many inconveniences that I would risk. As soon as the luck of the weapons is again in England's favor, such a move will surely draw the irreconcilable hate of England to me and the trade of my states. The only possibility which could be of use to the convictions of the colonies would be to send our wares on Dutch ships. We will supply the Americans our linen, fabric, and woolen products in exchange for their tobacco and other items, over which you will communicate with my private finance adviser, Magusch, in order for you to determine which would best fit our manufacturers. Thereby would some sort of direct trade with the colonies be established. Thus, we would not anger them through an absolute and formal refusal, and if they do gain their independence one day, so can this commerce win an even greater expansion and bring my states a thousand advantages."

Regarding Lee's residence in Berlin, the king had no objections under the condition that he came incognito and did not reveal his true nature.

Schulenburg proceeded according to these royal specifications completely. He wrote on May 11 and 20 in reply to Lee's letter that his indication over the opening of trade relations between America and Prussia is based less on the present and much more on the future. At the moment, his desire for realization of these plans still encounters significant difficulties in the way; therefore, Lee might not rush his journey to Berlin, as he certainly has more urgent and more important business to take care of. But Lee, as if he did not understand this polite rejection, traveled in the middle of May with Stephen Sayre, a former London sheriff who accompanied him as secretary, via Munich, Vienna, and Dresden to Berlin and arrived on June 4.

Arthur Lee, a born Virginian (1740-1792) and belonging to an aristocratic plantation family, was educated in London and practiced as an attorney there. He stood in association with the most significant political characters and performed important services for his fatherland at the outbreak of the revolution. In the year 1775 he was appointed by the colony of Massachusetts as Franklin's successor as agent in London. Congress appointed him in December of the same year as a secret agent there and sent him in October of 1776, to the disapproval of Jefferson, with Franklin and Deane to Paris as commissioner. Lee was a man of moderate intellect, little knowledge, and still less tact and perception. But with all the greater overconfidence and vanity with which he belittled everyone else, he wanted to force himself into the foreground and play the first role everywhere. He mixed himself into everything and very often spoiled the success through his vain and pathological lust for distinction, which he could have attained with more restraint and calculation. He boasted in his letters to the Congress that he had accomplished the French arms and cash remittance as if there had been no Vergennes nor Beaumarchais. He had delayed the rapprochement of this kingdom to the United States through a hasty trip to Spain, and so he rushed now to Berlin, not humbled by the recent humiliation suffered in Bilbao, to complete an alliance with Prussia in any case, and shame his colleagues left behind in Paris through his success. They did not like him and tried to get rid of him, as a result of which they expedited his departure. Lee seemed so sure of his success that he even wrote to Franklin and Deane on May 27 while in transit from Vienna that they only need be concerned that both courts (Paris and Madrid) join Prussia in recognizing the American independence.[16]

---

16 Arthur Lee is shown here in an unfavorable light. However, he wrote pamphlets opposing slavery and British policies. He was also one of the country's first spies and responsible for exposing Bancroft.

As if all of these things hinged on the will of this commissar! Also Deane certainly mattered little in regards to these things as he had neither tact nor knowledge, had been duped by swindlers, and later even subsided from the cause of his fatherland. Franklin was a more significant diplomat, who even today, remains the greatest representative of the United States abroad. "A virgin state as ours," he had written as a warning to Lee in March 1777, "should always preserve its pure character and not run around seeking out alliances, but instead should await the application of others with dignity and decency." However, the warning, as we have seen, bore little fruit. Thanks to the connections that the Parisian envoy Lord Stormont and the Minister Suffolk had through the spy Bancroft,[17] whose friend was Silas Deane, the English ministry was as well informed about the actions and the intentions of the American agents in Paris as the Americans themselves. So, Suffolk could already inform his newly appointed envoy Hugh Elliot in Berlin of Lee's departure and plans on May 9, 1777. Elliot received assurance from Hertzberg and Finckenstein that the enemy of England would find neither protection nor asylum in Berlin. But despite all the external testimonials of friendship, Elliot was doubly on his guard, as he ascertained that one of the confidants of the king, Major von Zegelin (earlier envoy in Constantinople), was drawn to Lee in the hotel and conferred secret discussions with him there. Schulenburg accepted Lee's first communications on July 5.[18]

Naturally, these covered the advantages of trade with America

17 Edward Bancroft, a former pupil of Silas Deane, was a double agent during the war.

18 The Diplomatic Correspondence of the American Revolution, Vol. II, 66.

and the manner of its operation, with the latter being hindered, particularly by the 40-50 percent increased insurance premium as a result of the war. At the same time, Lee enclosed a list of especially beneficial items. A rifle, he explained, which cost 22 francs in Berlin, can be sold in America for 50 francs, and with this money, one can buy 200 pounds of tobacco there, which would bring 200 francs in Europe. The best means for the ships to be equipped is via the island of Sint Eustatius, then head directly for the American coast with a skilled captain at the helm and enter the nearest American port under the pretext that he had been driven off course by storms and had no more water. The danger is not great on the outward journey, and on the return journey one can easily know if the coast is safe. It will not be difficult to find a fine captain strong in the English language in Emden or Hamburg. At first, it would be better to send the ships to the trade agents of the United States who are employed in every major port such as Newburyport, Salem, and Boston in Massachusetts; New-London in Connecticut (Rhode Island, New York, and Philadelphia were in the hands of the English at the time); Baltimore in Maryland; York, Hampton, and Alexandria in Virginia; Charleston in South Carolina and Savannah in Georgia. He will write to the local agents that they are to grant the Prussian trade every easement imaginable in that port.

Schulenburg found it in accordance with the king's most important desire for American tobacco. In Prussia, the cultivation of this plant was significantly inhibited and absolutely not suitable to sell if it was not mixed with Virginian or Marylander tobacco. It was important to him to obtain American tobacco as cheaply as possible and, in this way, gain an advantage over the other states which cultivate the same commodity. As a supplement to the provided information, he requested a memorandum about the places where and at what premium one could insure the ships bound for America. Then he would consider Lee's proposals and let him know if he considered it possible to attempt them with any prospect of success.

The king replied to Schulenburg on June 10 from Mockrau: "I gather from your report that Mr. Lee, one of the plenipotentiaries of the English colonies in America currently situated in Paris, has arrived in Berlin. I fully agree with your attitude towards him. You have done very well not to indulge him too much. It is much more suitable that he first forms his proposals over the opening of trade with his homeland. However, I want to tell you in advance that I never will pay an insurance premium of 50 percent, which may serve as a guideline for your negotiations."

Lee didn't wait too long to reply. He answered Schulenburg on June 10, 1777, that, directly before his departure from Paris, the insurance premium for ships destined for America had been 12.5% in Cadiz and 40% in Bordeaux for the round-trip journey. At that time, the intention was to set up significant and responsible insurance companies in Rouen and Nantes, but he feared that only French property could be insured by them. Therefore, it would probably be best to attempt the insurance in Amsterdam, where 40% for the round-trip would prove an irresistible temptation. If the insurance to America is taken out in Berlin, Congress can take out the return insurance. This measure is opposed by the grievance that the latter has no cash funds to cover the possible losses. The trade of America with Europe is very discouraged, particularly through the export ban of weapons and munitions, which are essential to the defense of American Independence. Also, because it is exposed to the enemy since European ports are closed to the American warships, which consequently could not escort the merchants. With these and a thousand other difficulties and delays that Europe's current cautious system subjected the United States to, England found every possible opportunity to pull all trade to themselves again. But through their unfair and unwise policies, they abandoned America and presented it to the rest of Europe. An open acceptance of this offer would have immediately decided the matter. "I do not venture," Lee concludes his letter, "to question the wisdom of that policy which prefers the possibility of a gleaning of our fields after they have been devastated by a rented[19] and enraged enemy over the certainty of a full harvest from pristine land. Evidently, there are better reasons than are known to me. But it seems clear to me that if American trade, depending on the circumstances, is of no use nor harm to the European nations, it could give England no better opportunity to exclude them from it forever by restoring their monopoly or, with mercenary arms, reducing the American resources through destruction of the cities and devastation of the country. We are like Hercules in the cradle; we have been left alone to wrestle the serpent which plagues all of Europe."

On June 18, Schulenburg admitted that despite the high insurance premiums, the commerce between Prussia and America would be extremely beneficial for both sides, with the high prices of German wares and the cheap cost of American staple goods. But an almost insurmountable difficulty was that Prussia lacked ships, captains, and sailors to even attempt the opening of such a trade connection. The Prussian merchants, he said, can, at most, reach the coast. One must see if one can find ships in Holland or Hamburg that will take Prussian wares to America and if they can arrange insurance for the loaded cargo. Regarding these points, he

19 Referring to the hiring of German troops by England.

first wanted to make sure of them and then can make use of Lee's instructions as soon as they were done to his satisfaction.

Lee retorted on June 20 that the difficulties are not as great as Schulenburg has presented. The simplest and best way to initiate the desired connection is to allow American privateers[20] into the Prussian ports and provide them with everything they need there so they can sell their prizes and buy Prussian goods. It only required that the king give the American privateers this permission. Otherwise, their prizes taken in the north must be sold either in America or in more southerly ports where they are allowed to enter. In ten days, he would leave Berlin. Until then, he hoped to receive a decision from the minister about this important subject.

Schulenburg answered, forthwith but elusive, polite but vague, raising hopes but committing to nothing. Meanwhile, on June 21, he provided the king with a detailed report about Lee's latest request, which concerned the unhindered entry of American ships and privateers into Prussian ports, and suggested to be informed by the envoys in Paris about the guidelines that the French and Spanish governments followed for authorization of American ships into their ports. The king was in agreement, especially since he did not want what Lee requested. "I can not recognize the cleverness and discretion enough," he wrote on June 23, 1777, from Potsdam to Schulenburg, "which you have demonstrated in your reply to the American agent, Lee. We must proceed in the same tone and tell him that despite my fondness for his clients and himself that I, in order to support them, could not have a run-in with

20 'Privateer' refers to a private individual or ship commissioned by governments or authorities to carry out hostilities at sea. This is known as 'caper' in German. The term 'piracy' is sometimes used in negative connotations, but privateers are sanctioned by law. 'Prize' refers to vessels, equipment, or cargo that is captured in the act.

England."

"After I indicated to you," replied Schulenburg on June 26, 1777, to the persistent Lee, "in my letter from the 18th of our desire for the establishment of more direct trade relations with the American colonies, in which I set out the prerequisite that we overcome the obstacles in the way, all that remains is to answer your letter from 20th regarding the free admission of your privateers in our ports. I can assure you that the king would very gladly oblige your clients, but on the other hand, he can not offend the court of London under the present circumstances. Also, our ports have hitherto only received merchants, while they never are visited by warships, so our port officials would find themselves embarrassed at the unfamiliarity with the observed procedures. Therefore, we want to be informed of the formalities that France and Spain observe towards your cruisers and how they reconcile your free admission in their ports with their friendship for England. The result of your information will decide on what conditions we will give the desired permission." At the same time, Schulenburg wrote on June 30, 1777, to the Prussian envoy Goltz in Paris and asked for instruction about the latter point, but received only the answer that the stated powers turned a blind eye here and there. They may not permit any privateers of warring parties into their ports on the grounds of the Peace of Utrecht.[21] Therefore, proper permission has not been given to them.

The king posed no objection to these steps at this time, simply to advance the discussions. Any doubt which could have existed over this intention was most strikingly refuted by him. "We now have the American envoy here," he wrote on June 17, 1777, to his

21 Series of treaties settling the War of the Spanish Succession.

brother, Prince Heinrich,[22] "who has proposed a trade agreement to us. I plan to drag out these negotiations in order to land myself on the side which professes good fortune. I completely believe that lies in our best interests. The French charge us 200,000 Thalers to take our goods and drop them off in Pennsylvania."[23]

As far as the American gentlemen are concerned," continued Frederick on June 25, 1777, "I have forgotten to notify them that, regarding the request to use the port of Emden for their privateers, under no conditions could be granted without openly falling out with England. We can pursue the trade with America only with loss because the insurance premiums rose to 50 percent, thereby exhausting the whole profit which we could make with these colonists. But these people cannot dispense with us because there are many wares such as wool and linen products that we can sell to them cheaper than all the rest of Europe, in exchange for their tobacco, indigo, and sugar. At the moment, we are restricted to vending those goods to the French merchant navy, which they will then transport to the new continent, so that we do not offend anybody and can take advantage of the opportunity presented to us without uproar."

The less the king did and was willing to do for the Americans, the more he exhibited the friendliest interest in their outcomes during the whole of 1777. Solely to anger the English, he never called the Americans 'rebels,' which they certainly must be in his eyes. He always spoke most honorably and appreciatively of them at open table. In contrast, he always spoke very contemptuously about the 'goddamn Islanders,' the English generals and ministers. In this contempt, the king even lapsed into bad taste. It was

22 Prince Henry of Prussia, Frederick's younger brother, was suggested as the monarch for the U.S. in the "Prussian Scheme."

23 Oeuvres de Frédéric le Grand, Vol. XXVI, 374 & 393.

not a good joke, in any case, when he wrote to Voltaire on June 17, 1777, that every barking dog speaks the name Howe (pronounced Hau). On Oct 5, 1777, in a recipe that he shared with his friend d'Alembert for the bite of mad dogs, the king said that one should also use it against the English parliament because it was just as irrational – as if it had been bitten by a mad dog. "You will," he continued, "be at war with these Goddamns, the colonies will become independent, and France will recover the previously snatched-away Canada."

Still more definite and, in any case, more to the point, the king writes in a letter to d'Alembert on August 13, 1777, "Do you want to know," he writes, "what I think of the attitude of the English? What the whole world thinks of it. They have acted against good faith by not keeping their agreements with the colonies, and by declaring war at the wrong time and against the rules of wisdom. In the wake, this has only caused misfortune for them because they misjudged the colonies' power in a mindless way and imagined that General Gage can subdue them with his 5000 or 6000 men. They have taken additional troops into their service without thinking about the ships that will take them to America (the king here alludes to the fact that the first Hessian and Braunschweiger corps found no transport ships on their arrival at the port, losing the English four costly weeks). They have bought provisions and supplies on the London markets for an army that must fight in Pennsylvania. In short, there is hardly an error these Islanders did not commit. Why have they separated the corps of Carleton and Burgoyne by a distance of 300 miles? How can these corps provide mutual assistance at such a distance? Must they fall out with the Russians, alienate the Dutch through arrogance and impertinence, and increase the number of their enemies through their bad actions? But the thick veil that shrouds the future covers my eyes just as good as it does with others. If I wanted to foresee, according to the example of Cicero, what certain combinations seem to announce, I would perhaps dare to say that the colonies have to become independent because the current campaign certainly does not put them down, because the 'Goddamn' government will have trouble picking the pockets of private individuals for the means to bring about the next campaign, and because war will be declared by next spring between France and England and they will defeat England in the colonies together."

In a letter from Nov 3, 1777, to his brother Prince Heinrich, the king first mentioned the rumor from Paris of Burgoyne's defeat, which the English government suppressed. Then he continued, "We find ourselves, it seems to me, in the position of German actors who go to the French theater during their holiday to see their French colleagues play and then model themselves after their example. We observe Washington, Howe, Burgoyne, and Carleton to learn this great art of war from them, wherein one can never learn enough, laugh about their stupidities, and endorse what they carry out according to the laws of this art. His British Majesty and his ministers sit in the first row, but we are in paradise, and our hissing counts for nothing here. Lord Bute, the author of the play, should be hanged in the last act to make the performance more moving. Three acts have already been performed, so this great man could serve as jewelry for an English gallows at the end of 1779. But I think it is all the same to you, my brother, if Bute is hanged or not. I also truly do not know why I have entertained you with these trifles, and only chance has brought me onto these 'Goddamns.'" "The English," commented the king at another point, "have always lacked skill and flexibility in their negotiations with other nations. With greed, they sacrifice their own interests. They do not understand how to flatter others, and imagine that they can achieve anything through offers of money."

The evidence for this irritated mood of the king against the "islanders" could easily be multiplied. His bitterness against England increased wherever possible, especially due to the outbreak of the English hostilities with Holland.

However, to resume the thread of the narrative here, a sensational incident occurred on June 26, 1777, in Berlin, which the American agent tried to exploit in his own interest if possible. Lee sat at the table in his guesthouse, "Hotel Corsika" (Brüderstraße 2), when the English envoy opened his room by means of a servant with a skeleton key. They broke into the desk inside and stole a portfolio. By chance, Lee left the table earlier than usually and encountered Elliot on the stairs on the way to his room. Elliot was a highly inept thief because when he heard that the robbery victim hurried to complain to the police, he was seized by fear and bewilderment. Instead of bringing his plunder to safety to study it thoroughly, he got rid of it immediately, and the papers were found in front of Lee's door after barely half an hour. "At the police interrogation," writes Lee on June 29 and July 6 to Franklin and Deane, "it turned out that the servant of the English envoy was repeatedly offered 2000 ducats for Lee's papers. The envoy, likewise interviewed, stated that he wanted to immediately send for his servant so that he could account for himself. However, the servant did not appear. I could not determine if the stolen documents were read. I can hardly believe so, for I would certainly not have regained them if someone had known their contents. My journal also was found underneath, which included all of our discussions with Spain and France."

Already on June 28, 1777, Hertzberg reported the account of this incident to the king. Frederick wrote by hand under the document the words: "This is called a public theft. One would do well to ban this man from the court, but I do not want to pursue this to the utmost. Someone must advise him to take soothing remedies and at least four times per year to let the veins." The king spoke likewise in a letter to his brother, Prince Heinrich, about this affair. "A strange story has occurred in Berlin," he wrote on June 29, 1777. "In the absence of the American agent Lee, the English envoy went into his hotel and had taken his portfolio. But he became fearful and, without opening it, threw it on the steps of the guesthouse. All of Berlin is talking about the incident. I acted as if I knew nothing about it. If one wants to take severe action, one must ban this man (Elliot) from the court because he committed a public theft. But to avoid making noise, I suppressed the matter. However, I will not refrain from writing to England about it, so that these people at least know that it could have been handled less forgiving than I have, because it really is shameless."[24]

Frederick spoke less bitter on July 1 in a briefing issued to his London envoy, Count Maltzan. "I have responded to Mr. Elliot," he said after he had cited the story and excuses given to Minster Hertzberg, "that I have every reason to be disgruntled over an incident of this manner and his conduct, and that I find myself in the right if I demand someone involved with the committed fault to stand punishment. But I will exempt him from this with the expectation that in the future he shows more restraint and discretion in his steps and gives no more instigation or irregularities. Elliot thanked me for this generous response, but at the same time explained to my minister that he feared he had lost my trust and that of his own court through his rashness. Hence, he will give a

24 Oeuvres de Frédéric le Grand, Vol. XXVI, 394-395.

detailed and sincere report to the latter so that in London they can decide whether to recall him or if he should leave. The school of Bute forms such pupils!" Alongside his briefing, the king added privatim, "Oh this worthy student of Bute, this incomparable man, your goddamn Elliot! Truly the English should blush from the disgrace that they send such an envoy to foreign courts!"

Elliot excused himself to the English Ministry by saying that, during the course of the conversation at the table, he had let the statement slip that he would gladly pay a significant sum to the one who would bring him the papers of the rebel agents. Elliot told the same version to the Prussian ministers. Due to the royal handling of the matter, Hertzberg and Finckenstein were polite enough not to question the English emissaries further about the strange coincidence of his presence in the hotel when the theft was committed, nor about the accused servant. Elliot's explanation was pointless. Lord Suffolk, the foreign minister, gave Elliot a clear reprimand on August 1. "The statement which you have declared to your panel," he wrote, "as explainable as it may be in the heat of the conversation, was completely inappropriate coming from the mouth of an envoy of the court who always keeps to his honor and restrains himself from walking the crooked paths of deviousness and treachery. Even the mere desire which prompted the act through already frowned upon discussions is double reprehensible to a court that at this time proceeds with the utmost openness and friendship towards His Majesty as well as in fair appreciation of his own royal character."[25] Incidentally, this scolding seemed not to be taken too seriously because, on October 7, Suffolk presented the evidence that the reprehensible circumstances of these dealings can be overlooked because of the loyal zeal Elliot has shown. Elliot was sent the sum of 1000 pounds sterling to cover the

25 St. P.O. Prussia, Vol. 407.

extraordinary expenses for an operation that, "without unsuitable disclosures on his part, it could not be achieved, and would not have been justified, even at the most resounding success."

Lee's negotiations with Schulenburg so far had not got off the mark. So, he hoped now that a keen interest in himself had been awakened due to Elliot's ineptitude. Also, to win capital from the incident, he tried his luck directly with the king. On June 29, he submitted a memorandum, with the hardly believable naivety of a self-conceited beginner, to the experienced royal statesman that summarized all of his desires and genuine interests. He also tried to clarify national and international law. The letter is so characteristic of the writer that it does not deserve to be communicated here, based on its essential contents. One can envisage the 64-year-old victorious king who helped make history and international law and the 36-year-old inexperienced American advocate who had only just put down Smith, Grotius, and Vattel[26] after he copied a couple of quotes and learned national economics, politics, and history from them!

"Your realm has blossomed through your extraordinary wisdom," Lee wrote to the king, "thus the number and the prosperity of your subjects always still increases. No sentence is truer than that the riches of the king hinges on the number of their subjects. Ancient and modern history teaches that commerce is the father of the population. I need not specify evidence to one of the most learned kings who have ever lived. It is fact, and the reasons for this fact are obvious. The king who wishes to increase the number of his subjects as much as possible, should also expand and encourage trade in his land. Your kingdom is suited most excellently for that. The three great rivers that flow through it offer the greatest facilitation for commerce. It demands only a sufficiently

26 Notable minds in the realm of political theory and law at that time.

distant destination to train sailors and an extensively rich country to establish and maintain commercial relations. One such country is America. The recent events have snatched away England's monopoly on trade. Those nations which will now help a young and grateful nation against their oppressor and can thereby commit, can again reap profits from the American trade. While those that first wait for the close of the war will drive no commerce on their old paths. Thus, it is the most opportune moment for you to get involved in the American trade. It is true that you have no warships to defend the honor of your flag, but on the other hand, you possess, Sire, the best regiments in the world. England will not be so blind as to compel Your Majesty to unite these ferocious regiments with the forces of his enemies. Also, England is so weak and exhausted at the moment due to the American war that it must close its eyes to much worse measures. Secondly, it is said to not be practical to have such a large army as Your Majesty and an attention-demanding fleet at the same time because the latter requires too many enlisted men and will drive the country to its ruin. The rationale that if the population was reduced through trade, it would be increased by it would be right. It would put you in the position of possessing a great army, for experience teaches us that trade-driving nations always have the most numerous populations because they grow in proportion to the means of existence. Commerce so lifts your country. Thirdly, you need sailors for such an undertaking. Maritime trade itself generates them. If Your Majesty's ports were open to our armed ships so that they may enter unhindered to deliver their cargo, to be repaired, and could secretly sell their prizes, so would your seafarers be given instruction and encouragement. And especially if they were given permission to make a journey in our ships, seafarers would emerge out of your subjects in a shorter time and sailors from other countries would stream into your ports with the intention to cruise in the American waters. Perhaps some will say that such participation would decide the issue of the American independence. But this is not so."

Lee then sought to demonstrate that the United States is independent and that according to international law, neutral nations only had to adhere to the fact, not to the law. It is also thus according to English law. England had recognized the Duke of Braganza as King of Portugal in 1641 on the grounds that he was summoned to the crown by the unanimous wish of the people. The American Congress derives its power entirely from the same source. In 1608, France met with the duke Karl von Suedermanland as king of Sweden in negotiations because it benefited Henry IV's interests and his kingdom. "The example of the great Henry is one worthy of a ruler, who has no small claim to the name of 'the Great.'" Finally, Vattel is quoted. "The benefits which will blossom from Your Majesty's states commerce with America will be very great. It will give them a new push and will grow with the population of America. We will send them tobacco, indigo, cotton, and furs in exchange for their cloth, linen, porcelain, and ironware. These profits would indeed be greatly decreased through devastation by the English and their mercenaries if we must carry on through the war alone against all their forces with our lack of weapons and munitions. It falls to Your Majesty, in community with some other European powers, to stop this devastation through a commercial alliance with our United States. There is no more revered name to us than Your Majesty's, and there is, of course, no king whose declared friendship would lend our people so much courage and our cause so much strength."

Before a reply to this letter could follow, Lee asked the king on July 1 for a private audience to lodge and make public his complaint against Elliot, which he dared not entrust to documents. But Frederick informed him in a note from July 2 that Schulenburg would receive all of his information and that a steadfast silence should be observed regarding it. Of course, that was not what Lee had wanted. But since his desire for a personal audience with the king would not materialize, he engaged the minister on July 3. After he first painted a rosy picture of the resources of America and unleashed a lament about its abandonment by the great European powers, he requested mainly a supply of guns – both rifles and sidearms, bullets and powder, to be transported to America under Prussian flag via Sint Eustatius or St Croix and would be paid in tobacco, rice or indigo. If the king should not want to consent to this plea, Lee desired a 6 percent loan of two million pounds sterling or 13 million Prussian Thalers, or as much as one should find suitable. He could not offer other collateral as the means for this loan to bring about the independence of the United States. However, should this latter event occur, it would become a sacred national debt, which could be paid off with the country's products at beneficial prices. The king writes in the margin of the report to his minister the words: "Such proposals are unacceptable. They would surrender our affairs to chance without that we could ever expect a reliable benefit from it."

Schulenburg apologetically informed the corresponding Lee that such a request was denied, who incidentally seemed to have expected a negative answer and only asked for his clients' sake. On the other hand, he gave Lee a copy of the judicial discussions about the theft of the English envoy, at his request, and gladly approved the requested permission to report over the course of the

American war. At the minister's request, the king had explained that the more favorable the news was to the American cause, the more fond he would welcome it. Lee was also allowed to buy rifles and fabric for uniforms in Prussia and ship them via Szczecin or Hamburg. In the meantime, the foreign minister rushed to assure the English envoy that these goods were in the market for the highest bidder, so their sale could not be viewed as a special favor.

As he had finally realized that his efforts were unsuccessful, Arthur Lee departed again for Paris on July 10 and arrived there at the end of the month. At that time, England had raised objections against the arrival of American privateers in French ports and obtained a strict ban against it from the Versailles cabinet. Under the pretext that it would be impossible to obtain sailors in America for merchant ships at the high profit that privateering yielded (which existed primarily in the imagination of the agent), Lee again requested on August 13, 1777, that the American privateers be granted refuge in Emden. The king offhandedly wrote on September 6 in this letter submitted to him in translation by Schulenburg: "He wants to enter our ports, that won't do. This has already been refused to him." But before Schulenburg could communicate the casual rejection, a second letter from Lee arrived. He writes on September 21 that he awaits the minister's reply with great suspense, and also presents Franklin's reasons why it would be extremely advantageous for the European states and capitalists to lend money to the United States. At a rate much more beneficial than if they gave it to England. "The king," answered Schulenburg on Oct 8, 1777, "despite his good wishes for you, has deemed it not fitting to permit your privateers free entry into his ports at a time when even France, despite the significant gain that it derives from the trade with America, has given in to the protests of the English ministry. We must wait for more convenient circumstances to establish a trade connection between both nations, the development of which will greatly delight His Majesty, until it does not compel you to make moves that stand in contradiction with your principles. I find your memorandum very well written. It will certainly not fail to leave its impression on those countries who speculate in loans with enemy nations. It should please me to hear more about the state of affairs in America from you."

Lee's response to the king's "reject with compliments"-based cabinet order was an extremely cool but polite letter that was as clumsy as possible, and would surely have ended the correspondence with the Prussian minister for good if not for the possibility of receiving reliable news from America to perhaps use against England. "It would have pleased me," writes Lee among other things on October 23, "if His Majesty would have given an example to the rest of Europe, instead of him receiving it from them. It is not good that the fearful lead the brave or that the weak directs the wise. Convinced of His Majesty's friendlier attitude towards the United States, I hope that the motives that oppose its more open declaration will not outlast the surety that our enemy cannot wrest the sword from us, despite all efforts of whose handling is the strongest argument for our independence." At the same time, Lee asked Schulenburg if the United States had to fear new recruit shipments from Russia, Germany, and Denmark and asked the minister to make his own contribution to the thwarting of such plans. Schulenburg reassured him about the latter point on November 6 that no foreign troops would be sent to America except for several hundred German recruits. He also requested detailed and immediate information regarding the rumors from America penetrating Europe about Howe's entry into the

Chesapeake Bay and Burgoyne's defeat. "The king is pleased about each of your cause's favorable events and will hear confirmation of the latest rumors with special enjoyment. Give me thus reliable details, since it is very difficult to trust the verity of reports as the greater portion of them are made up and released in the interest of some party." However, on November 28, Schulenburg declined a reception by the king of William Lee (brother of Arthur),[27] who was entrusted with a mission from Congress, because the state of affairs in Berlin had not changed in the least since the visit of the latter. On the other hand, there was nothing against him coming as a private citizen to Berlin and promised on December 23 to notify the new agents as soon as the king deemed it feasible to begin negotiations. William Lee never came to Berlin under these circumstances. Instead, he corresponded with Schulenburg from Frankfurt am Main, Paris, or Brussels. William was altogether more tactful than and not as conceited as his brother Arthur and thus was not without diplomatic dexterity as a result. His letters distinguish him through objectivity and warm patriotism. He spotted the smallest advantages to favor his countrymen wherever possible and used them happily for his purposes. To such effect that Finckenstein praised him as a skilled diplomat, and Schulenburg gave him his personal trust and sincere attention.

The American agents perceived the Prussian minister's solicitation for more frequent reporting as an indirect encouragement of their cause and quickly bombarded him with more ideas, suggestions, and requests. Carmichael brought the shipment of tobacco again to the talks, which, he reckoned, could be landed

27 William Lee served as a diplomat in Austria and Prussia. He was also appointed as Sheriff of London while serving as an agent for the Virginia tobacco trade there. He was Sheriff the same year as the aforementioned Stephen Sayre.

in a Prussian or Swedish port. He stated that the Prussian manufactures were 25% cheaper than the French and noted that he had obtained 47,000 pounds sterling for the former. 'Just some encouragement,' he concluded his letter from December 6, 1777, 'for the granting of the secret arrival of our privateer in Emden, and a splendid business will develop!' Schulenburg replied that he would gladly be prepared to take 200,000 pounds of tobacco in Emden, but submitted that they had no ships in America. Arthur Lee also shared a letter with Schulenburg at the beginning of December from a third brother, the congressman Richard Henry Lee, who remarked that a port for the American privateers in the north of Europe would be of much use to both powers since it will be impossible to send American products on merchant ships from America to Europe. On December 11, Arthur Lee sent a comprehensive report about Howe and Burgoyne. According to American sources, he reduced the inflated English depiction of Howe's success and told of Burgoyne's defeat.

Schulenburg presented a translation of these letters and reports to the king on December 15, as they were of general interest, whereupon he wrote back by his own hand, "That is all very nice, but you must tell him that I intend to recognize the independence of the United States when France has done the same." Schulenburg replied on December 18, "I am very pleased about this good news. Judging by your description of the situation, even more significant events can be expected before the end of the campaign or even during the winter. I hope you will submit all of your incoming authentic reports to me without delay. The king, who receives your news very graciously and expresses his satisfaction thereon, will not be the last power to recognize your independence as soon as it is to your favour. Meanwhile, you must realize that would not be the case if he were the first, but that France, whose political and trade interests are more tightly connected with yours, should set the example."

Arthur Lee immediately sought to pull practical benefits from this favorable mood towards his cause and asked Schulenburg on December 28 if he could buy rifles in Prussia because he very much desired to introduce Prussian weapons into the United States army. The king had objections against this. "Since the events of the war become more interesting with each day, so must I repeatedly request," wrote the minister to Lee on January 16, 1778, "that you constantly communicate your detailed reports to me. The king himself takes a lively interest in them and wishes that your noble endeavors may be crowned with success. As I have already notified you by letter on December 18, he will not hesitate to recognize your independence as soon as France, who is involved to a much higher degree in this war, has preceded by example. In addition, His Majesty would not set the slightest difficulties in the way of your ships' arrival in Prussian ports if you had a fleet that could avenge an affront to one of your ships. As safe as it is, the harbor of Emden does not have a fort for its defense. For these reasons, the king does not want to be exposed to unpleasant consequences. You can buy as many weapons and rifles as you want. The bankers Splittgerber (tenant of the rifle factory) have received instruction to provide you with what you require. I have enclosed a price list." Over the summer, Lee ordered 800 rifles at 6 Thaler, 15 Silbergroschen (schilling)[28] per piece, and shipped them through the House de Chapeaurouge[29] in Hamburg to

28 Prussian currency of the time; 1 Thaler= 30 Silbergroschen, 1 Silbergroschen= 12 pfennig.

29 Family of French origin that became very influential in Switzerland and also in Hamburg as members of the 'Hanseatics,' the ruling class of the city.

Bordeaux but claimed to have been cheated by Splittgerber. Upon closer investigation, this proved untrue. In October, he turned to Schulenburg for compensation – an outrageous imposition that the minister curtly rejected.

At that time, the looming of the War of the Bavarian Succession (January 3, 1778 – March 13, 1779)[30] and the outbreak of war soon after designated a turning point in the policies of the king regarding England and America, which now dropped the previously formed connections with the agents of Congress. In the North of Germany, he was again reliant on the same allies who had stood beside him during the Seven Years War; at least they might not confront him with hostilities or threaten to stab him in the back. It is only for this reason that he pulled on more polite strings with the king of England and appeared cold and rejecting towards the Americans. Nevertheless, the agents, especially William Lee, did not lessen their insistence on recognition. Even though the negotiations became more hopeless on the German side almost daily, they still dragged on for the next three years due to American perseverance and tenacity. The content of the demands and the form of the rejection always remained the same; thus, the following account of the communication of the correspondence's essential points is justifiably limited. William Lee had asked Schulenburg on January 16, 1778, if he may come to Berlin and enter into formal negotiation. The minister sent this letter to the king on January 31. However, the king replied through his cabinet order on February 1, 1778, that he must reject entering into formal negotiations at the current state of affairs, as good as the proposition of William Lee might be to him. On March 20, 1778, Lee reported that France had recognized the United States

30 Basically a power struggle conflict between Austria and Prussia, the high casualties from disease and starvation earned it the name "Potato War."

and tied to it the hope that the king of Prussia must now surely deem the moment to be right for him (Lee) to travel to Berlin. Frederick replied to this view on March 30 that at the moment he was so busy with Germany that he could not think about America and would gladly recognize it as independent. However, at this time, it yielded them no benefits and could only damage Prussia. Nevertheless, Lee was undeterred, despite Schulenburg having communicated this answer and had informed him that the king would depart for the theater of war very soon and would not be able to converse. On April 18, Lee asked if he may come to Berlin to finally conclude the proposed agreement on his way to Vienna, where he was going as the Congress's authorized representative. The king, after Schulenburg had presented this letter, decreed on April 27 from the headquarters at Schönwalde bei Frankenstein in Silesia, "You can answer the American William Lee on his request that the colonies, even if I now recognized them, would have no advantage from it since I possess no fleet to protect their trade. Thus, such a measure on my side cannot be asserted as it is not suitable, and he would encounter the same difficulties at the Vienna court. Not land powers, such as Austria and myself, can help you in any way, but rather it is the naval powers that are in a position to get involved in maritime affairs. It seems to me to lie in your interest to pull Holland, Spain, and Denmark to your side, but not powers that you could expect no help from. That is all that I have to say to you regarding this issue." A couple of days later, the king received Lee's detailed information about the state of affairs in America through Schulenburg and replied on May 4, "I see from your report from April 30 that you have answered the American Lee according to my instructions. I have also found confirmation of the favorable news regarding the American cause in the letter from 24th of last month. I must confess that it is wonderful, and I thank you for this communication, as local affairs preoccupy me infinitely more than those."

Lee continued with his reports. On July 17, he even renewed his inquiry asking if the king still did not consider it appropriate for him to come to Berlin now to fulfill his orders. In any case, he wished to be notified about whether one of the American merchant ships is granted free trade in the ports of His Majesty and whether one of the American privateers is allowed to enter this port merely to buy necessary provisions. In response to this, in an exceptionally written cabinet order on July 30, 1778, in German, the king summed up yet again his view of the matter: "With regards to the Americans, you (Schulenburg) need only write again the same that I have already said ten times. In particular, that I have no fleet and so could not get involved nor cover my ports. Thus, I cannot allow enemy ships to enter my ports because they could be seized by their enemies without that it could be prevented. This is not something for me. Anyhow, you must see to dismiss it in a polite manner."

Now, Lee limited his letters from August 28 and October 31, 1778, again to political coverage. On December 1, he sought to win Schulenburg over by proposing the king of Prussia as arbitrator for the conclusion of the American war. He also asked that American merchants, like the ships of other nations, may enter into Emden and exchange their products for Prussian wares there. He also demanded that the king protect the American vessels and that he should reclaim them if they would be taken by another power. Initially, Schulenburg absolutely did not dare to submit this petition to the king, who had already shown to be very disgruntled about the eternal request. Finckenstein, to whom the Minister of

Commerce turned for council in his predicament, advised him to file the report to Frederick since the concealment of this petition could be interpreted badly, and since his attention was directed on the matter anyway since Colonel Arendt, a born Stendaler who served in the American army, traveled to Breslau directly to headquarters with similar propositions. So, Schulenburg related it to the king, who in return informed his minister from Wroclaw on December 19 to reiterate to Mr. William Lee, "that we have neither ships nor frigates nor galleys to guard the entry into our ports. On these grounds, the trade of non-forbidden wares of all nations in my seaports is allowed, but I cannot understand how to guard the prizes made there since I lack a fleet."

On January 2, 1779, Schulenburg reported this to the agents and emphasized that the Americans required no more explicit permission than any other nation to come to Emden. Lee now handled to this point with great skill. "Since we, until now, are still not recognized as a nation by His Majesty," he said in his retort from January 30, 1779, "it seems necessary that the king either formally closes a treaty with us or that he delivers a positive declaration that he recognizes the United States as a nation." Now Schulenburg saw that his answer was not general enough. Although he viewed Lee's demand as fair, he dared not bother the king again with this annoying issue. In his perplexity, he again turned to Finckenstein on February 9. "Lee," replied Finckenstein on February 14, "is no clumsy negotiator. He wants to achieve through cunning what he could not attain directly. The granting of his demand would be synonymous with a recognition of the United States. Thus, we would be paraded and compromise ourselves at the London court. The king will never do that; therefore, you need not write to him all over again." Heeding this advice, Schulenburg wrote to Lee on February 17, 1779, that a new statement would be redundant since the king had already answered his letter from December 1, 1778, that the North American businessmen (as the above cabinet order from December 19 and Schulenburg's letter from January 2 referred to) who arrive with their ships in Prussian ports to trade in non-forbidden goods will be as well received and treated as the merchants of other nations. Lee must have been appeased by this assessment and even went so far as to excuse the misunderstanding due to his poor knowledge of the French language. Besides, he noticed that he had the permission for American merchants to enter Prussia. He immediately reported home. The correspondence ceased from then until after the termination of the War of the Bavarian Succession.

The War of the Bavarian Succession had more favorable consequences for England than for America. Frederick intentionally hurt England wherever possible and had disrupted their soldier trade with the German princes quite harshly at the end of the year 1777 and had damaged it badly by refusing the free passage of the rented troops. Even up until the year 1778, there was hardly any small or petty chicanery against England that the king had not permitted. At the end of November 1777, he issued a circular to the Prussian merchants, wherein he warned them to be especially cautious because the interruption of trade with the American colonies would result in significant bankruptcies in England, thus simultaneously leading to the fall of Dutch and Hamburg houses. Suffolk was beside himself and formally raged, "Now the dangerous opponent even attacks English commerce!" The English minister used particular expressions against the earlier "exalted allies," saying they belonged in a pub rather than in a ministerial correspondence, but he must swallow his anger. On December 27,

1777, even Elliot declared that Lee should be received in Berlin in entirely the same manner as Franklin and Deane in Paris. It was only diplomatic gossip, and only Suffolk believed it. "The king," continued Elliot, "retorted to a minister who sought to explain the impropriety of such a reception that America is an ascending star, an independent and powerful state whose friendship can be gained under easy terms, and he expects no inconveniences but rather great advantages from a connection which promises extremely profitable trade for his subjects. The king has mentioned the poor treatment which he received in the last war from England multiple times. His whole attitude shows the yearning wish to take vengeance on us."

Even at the beginning of 1778, when all plans to connect with the United States were already abandoned, Elliot still believed in their soon implementation. On January 10, he wrote, "On the instigation of his commerce minister and the numerous salaried Frenchmen in the Ministry of Commerce, the king plans to establish direct commerce between his realm and North America. He is convinced that the colonies will be independent and expects extraordinary advantages for his subjects in such a big market. A good harmony prevails between Prussia and France regarding the American colonies. The refused free passage should encourage the rebels; they have us to thank for this also. The worst consequences of the king's mood against England would be expected if not for the untimely death of the Elector of Bavaria, opening a new field for his restless ambition and again awakening his natural jealousy towards Austria."

These events now altered the state of affairs with a bang. The entanglements with the Emperor[31] claimed the complete attention of the king. England was now treated most considerately by him.

31 Joseph II, Hapsburg ruler of the Holy Roman Empire.

The first most insignificant result of these changes in Frederick's demeanor was that the poor devils whom England had put together through its German suppliers could again be hauled to the slaughterhouse in America without any objection.

The king's relationship to the mercenary trade has often been tendentiously distorted. Yet, it is not difficult to detect the concerns that guide him, mainly because he has frequently expressed them. He opposed the recruiting for England, not out of Utopian humanity, but rather out of much more sober calculations. His policies meant that he frustrated England's desires. Just because he has a peculiar policy, the great king of Prussia stands so proud and reverence-commanding opposite of these little German princes. He is the single German reigning monarch of that time who, because he feels personal responsibility in front of the world, also has personal dignity. The single reigning monarch who pursues great political goals with clear eyes and does not shy away from calling things by their right names with truly exalted impartiality. "If the Landgrave of Hesse had emerged out of my school," wrote Frederick to Voltaire on June 18, 1776, "he would not have sold his subjects to the English as one sells cattle to haul on to the slaughterhouse." On an earlier occasion at the beginning of his administration, when the Dutch rented troops from Braunschweig, the king had compared the buyer to a butcher who hikes to Podolia to trade in heavy oxen.[32] On the contrary, as already noted above, this is an anecdote invented by Franklin and retold at first by Koertum as a fact. It was eventually spread further uncritically by Johann George Schlösser and countless others that the Hessian soldiers had to pay the livestock tax at Minden on Frederick's

32 Comparing the German mercenaries to a group of cattle breeds from the Ukraine, which were known for being hardy, adaptable, and were most often used as draught animals.

orders because they were being sold like cattle. Schlösser printed this passage to his heart's delight in wide-spaced block letters.

The king's confident mockery and contempt that affected England and its suppliers everywhere is doubly agreeable because there were no independent politics in Germany apart from Prussia and the Emperor and because the remaining German states eked out their pitiful existence only through supple clinging to foreign interests. In the king's words and measures lies such a mental superiority over the little imperial princes that one can very well explain the jubilation of the oppressed and the joy of those not involved in the disgraceful trade. The people loved to attribute the best minds as their heroes, making them the bearers of their dearest hopes and wishes. So, it was based on a couple of cutting statements made in private letters or on the blackboard which denounced the stingy and greedy princes, that the hate of all thinking contemporaries against the sale of souls was embodied in Frederick, despite the fact that he never acted differently towards the acquisition of soldiers.

The sober historiography can only comprehend his relationship to this trade from the standpoint of his personal interests. The king initially had a very concrete wanting for the strongest army possible. This did considerable damage to the recruiting agencies of the smaller sovereigns. As long as the first negotiations were pending, a few thousand were expected at the most as a result—but not approximately 20,000 men. Nevertheless, no obstacles were placed in the way of the shipping of the main corps. Frederick did not become concerned until the autumn of 1777 that if the troop consignments to America progressed as they had previously, he would be short of his own requirements. He described his point of view himself, "The king of England negotiated with all courts of

Germany to draw the few people from them which are still able to be supplied. Germany already feels the aftermath of the numerous personnel deliveries which were sent to alien parts of the world. The King of Prussia is concerned that the realm would be robbed of its defenders in the event of a new war, for in 1756, Lower Saxony and Westphalia alone had brought an army to mount with which they could stop and thwart the French army's progress."

For this reason, he harassed the troops of the German princes who allied with England as soon as they passed through Magdeburg, Minden, and the territory of the Lower Rhine. It was weak revenge for the bad conduct that the court of London had observed against him regarding the city and the ports of Gdansk. Besides, the king did not want to push matters to the extreme because previous experience had taught him that one can always find enemies without having to draw them in out of cockiness.

Frederick acted from this point of view. On October 21, 1777, Suffolk had instructed his envoy, Elliot, for the incoming of Hesse-Hanau and Anspach recruits via unimpeded passage through the king's territory, not doubting that he only fulfills a formality with such a request since the king had always shown himself to be compliant and courteous on this point up until now. Elliot's astonishment was great when, at the beginning of November, he received an answer to his petition from Count Finckenstein, "that regardless of the wishes of His Prussian Majesty to demonstrate friendship at every opportunity to His British Majesty, you see yourself the necessity to refuse the request for the passage of troops destined for America through these states, and the disorder and troubles caused by similar transports in the past years forces His Majesty to no longer issue such a permission in the future." What mockery that Finckenstein, in verbal discussion with the

English envoys, added the proposition to this written answer – that the troops could reach the port of embarkation just as easily via a small detour and assured Elliot of the firm and unwavering friendship of the king for George III apart from this. The English minister made a second attempt directly to the king, who replied that he was sorry, but the refusal must hold, due to the stated reasons in his first notification. As Elliot's predecessor, James Harris, made his attendance before the king in Potsdam, the Chancellor, Cocceji, remained in the room and had an indifferent conversation with him, intentionally avoiding all political questions, so Harris had no opportunity to explain the purpose of his visit, let alone bring the conversation on America. Elliot was in the greatest quandary. He did not know how he should explain the negative response of the king. He guessed back and forth and relayed his concern in a letter to Suffolk, including many plausible reasons, and yet did not exhaust the matter. "Those who pretend to know the secrets of Potsdam," Elliot wrote on November 16, 1777, "claim that when the usual requests for free passage through Hanau and Anspach were submitted, the king had just read the report of his recruiting officers which complained about the difficulties of attaining their yearly quota. The reason attributed to this was that the troops had been shipped to America. Yesterday, it was communicated to me in trust that the king did not expect the recruitment of new corps and that he was prompted to give his disapproval through the negotiations of procuring troops taking place in Zerbst, so near to his borders. Although these circumstances might have had some weight, the king's position cannot be attributed to them alone, in my opinion. Instead, it must be the current general state of affairs and the more extensive views and plans of this enterprising monarch that are likewise thrown with into the weighing pan.

When his British Majesty undertook subsidy contracts with different German princes at the outbreak of the current unrest, none of them dared to conclude them without attaining the approval of the Berlin court beforehand. This was more willingly given since England had a certain degree of dependence on the plots of the sinister and scheme-concocting Potsdam Cabinet by doing so, and because his Prussian Majesty could completely stop or allow these essential reinforcements at will. You know about the Prussian king's connection with the rebel agents in Paris, whose misrepresentations about the state of our affairs at home and in America have contributed so much to lead the king's judgment astray. He frequently states his doubt about the success of our weapons and even declared once that, according to his view, we have lost our colonies. Sir William Howe's withdrawal from New Jersey prompted the perception that no decisive blow could be managed during the current war. His long silence confirmed this view, and the passage of the recruits was denied on the Prussian side before the latest good news came to Berlin. I am convinced that an intimate letter exchange with the rebels and false reports have had this effect and brought forth such an obvious switch in the attitude of the Berlin court. I say obvious because I am sure that the initial willingness only hides the real intentions of his Prussian Majesty, which aim to pull any and all possible advantages from England's embarrassments. If the news of Howe's and Burgoyne's decisive victories are authentic, so will the Berlin court undoubtedly return to its earlier system. On the other hand, if significant reinforcements should be required for service in the next few years, I fear we will realize great sacrifices. Allow me still the comment, that the king of Prussia would certainly not regret to see England involved in a war with the house of Bourbon in these critical moments. Russia stands in the notion to bridge the gap so that an alliance between Berlin and Vienna can arise on the same basis of separation which is already preserved and poses no obstacle in the way of either power. The outrageous measure that constitutes the object of this dispatch will make our enemies believe that our resources for the procurement of German mercenaries are very uncertain. Likewise, it will give great encouragement to the cabinet of Versailles."

Suffolk was no less embittered. He was spurred on by Prince Kaunitz, who himself had painted Frederick as the troublemaker of Europe, and as the agitator of France against England in the most blatant colors. Kaunitz – one thinks, Kaunitz! – successfully played the role of an honest man sick in his holiest emotions even towards the English, and wrote that the king's stance against England was "due to his constant contempt for more moral obligations!"[33] Suffolk, the English Minister of Foreign Affairs, poured out an extensive and mostly unjustified lamentation against Frederick to his Viennese envoy. "If proof was still missing for the ungrateful, treacherous and awful policies of this ruler," he wrote on November 14, 1777, to Sir R. M. Keith, "this fact shared to us now by Prince Kaunitz will be sufficient to fill us with every possible caution towards him. I consider it my duty to tell you that similar reports came to us that stand in harmony with that fact. For we know that this man has lowered himself to tread in direct communication with the rebel agents in Paris. At the same time as he stands in friendly relations with them, he indirectly supplies

33 Wenzel Anton, Prince of Kaunitz-Rietberg, was known as a clever master of diplomacy and politics. Mr. Kapp alludes here to the fact that Kaunitz himself had actually played the chief role of rearranging and agitating the alliances of Europe with the Treaty of Versailles and the Diplomatic Revolution, both in 1756.

troops against them whilst he encourages the subsidy contracts of a near branch of his house."

Suffolk alludes to the Margrave of Anspach, the nephew of the king who he thoroughly despised and, as was well known, treated him on the same footing as the Hessian and Zerbstian princes. As the English minister wrote this letter, he knew quite well that the Anspachian troops had been refused free passage through Prussian territory. His impotent rage let him distort even the most well-known facts. Nevertheless, Elliot continued to pour oil on the fire through his reports. In one of his latest conversations with Finckenstein on November 16, 1777, he stated he had noticed how desirable the continuance of good harmony between the kings of Prussia and England was. "Finckenstein replied that his Lord has only a single alliance which he strives to obtain. He meant the alliance with Russia, which the entire current political system of Prussia revolved around. So, should the king be influenced, it must occur through Russia. Each day, the king of Prussia misses no opportunity to superimpose his antipathy towards the king of England. Indeed, his bitterness breaks out on every occasion. Therefore, if we need him for the execution of our plans, it requires either tremendous sacrifice or enlisting Russia's help. Schulenburg recently expressed quite openly that the independence of America would be a great prize for Prussia, indeed for all of Europe."

Not long afterward, the first news of the capture of Burgoyne arrived via Paris. This excited all the more painful sensation in Berlin, since the Braunschweig corps under Officer Riedesel,[34]

34 Friedrich Adolf Riedesel, general who commanded all German troops leased by Britain during the Saratoga campaign, and is credited with introducing the Christmas tree to North America while in Canada after his release from capture.

son-in-law of the Prussian Minister, Massow, were affected by the sad fate. Most of the captured Braunschweig officers were known in Berlin and stood in friendly relations with their Prussian comrades since the Seven Years War. Therefore, this blow was felt more deeply and painfully in Berlin than some other misfortune. Burgoyne's inability was generally blamed for the difficult loss. "The permission for the passage of mercenaries was already drawn up," writes Elliot on November 29, 1777, "then came the news of Burgoyne's defeat, and the ban was imposed. Now every prospect of a favorable turnaround of the Prussian politics for us has diminished."

This ban dropped like a bomb among the affected English agents and German princes as well as their ministers. Upon hearing of the alleged disorder the ban was based on, Sir Joseph Yorke, the English envoy in the Hague, justifiably wrote to the English agent, Rainsford, on November 15, 1777, "Everyone has too holy a shyness before his Prussian Majesty and wavers before him in too much fear to lose men on the journey through his territory, as they would risk to perpetrate any displeasing act to the king." Express mail and couriers were immediately sent from one court to the other, notes were exchanged, and attempts made to the Prussian envoys in Cologne and the commanders of Wesel, asking them to turn a blind eye. But everything was in vain. "Until now," exclaimed Faucitt, the English negotiator, "the Rhine was open to the whole world. Now it has been unexpectedly and quickly closed. It is too late to change our route. The same interruption threatens in Minden. I have immediately written to Berlin, Hanau, Anspach, and Cassel. Schlieffen (the minister of the Landgraves) recommended taking the Weser River from Hesse to get around the Prussian territory." Cressener, the English envoy to the Electorate of Cologne, complains in like manner, "The troops cannot march in this country. Moreover, it is impossible not to pass through Prussian territory along the Rhine, and then the boats with the uniforms will certainly be stopped in Wesel." The Anspach Colonel Schlammersdorf complains in a letter from Bendorf on November 18, 1777, "If your court finds no means to change the decision of the king of Prussia, everything is lost, and we are ruined because it is absolutely impossible to march on land." Rainsford himself, who was already waiting for the new supply of troops in Nijmegen, found the delay to be so disagreeable since the transport ships had already arrived in Holland. The weather left nothing to be desired, and the troops could be shipped in a couple of days.

Here, good advice was also costly. They eventually helped themselves by taking it, and the Anspachers and Hanauers were quartered for the winter in Hanau and started their march to the Weser estuary at the end of February 1778. The 534 men had only arrived in Bremerhaven in the second half of March because they had to circumvent Prussian territory. The Zerbsters had to wait for the springtime before they went through Saxony, Braunschweig, and Hanover to Stade. But on their fortnightly march of that kind, they lost a number through desertion. Of the 841 men who stood at the flag on February 21, only 494 still remained on March 21, 1778.

One must visualize the then state of affairs in the American theater of war to properly appreciate the significant, if not decisive, consequences of the policies of Frederick the Great on the English war effort. After his miserable campaigns of the autumn of 1777, Washington remained in his winter quarters at Valley Forge from the middle of December until the middle of June 1778, exposed to all hardships of the season, suffering under all the abuses and deficiencies of a disorganized administration. Never until now, not even after the defeats of the summer and autumn of 1776, had the cause of the young Republic stood so bad, because never before had the spirit and strength of the nation been so humbled and discouraged. The ragged, starving, and freezing poor devils, who were hardly more than 5000 men strong, were introduced to the American army at the beginning of 1778 and were then first trained under Steuben in the rudiments of discipline. They were capable of no serious opposition if Howe had attacked them with a superior force. But the English general let the most opportune time to attack expire unused because, at this critical moment, he heard of Frederick's ban, which temporarily cut off any prospect of further reinforcements. It was not just the couple of hundred men whose delayed or canceled arrival that had hurt England so severely, but rather the uncertainty for the future, which excluded any safe calculation of aid and threatened to cut off the supply of German reinforcements for England. The importance of the policies of Frederick for the American war lies in this. They were worth as much as a new ally for Washington in their consequences. They granted him time and helped turn the luck in the war. Without wanting it, the king had shown a substantial service to the Republican generals and the young free states.

But to get back to Europe: from the moment that the War of the Bavarian Succession was certain, Frederick started to drop any kind of negotiations with the Americans. He approached England again with perhaps a little too much haste. In Potsdam for a visit in the middle of February, the hereditary prince of Braunschweig played the middle man. He assured Elliot in the name of the king that if an alliance between Prussia and France should come about as a result of the steps taken by the Imperial court in Bavaria, the strictest neutrality for the German possessions of the king of England would be fixed. Everything that has been told of Frederick's intrigues in Hannover and of his other discord against England springs from a class of people like Beaumarchais, in whose interest it was to spread such lies. On the contrary, the king wished to restore the old union of England with its colonies. When the last proposals about Emden were made to him, he rejected them with the remark that he did not want to attract serious entanglements by way of such trivialities. Then, in the first days of March, the king also allowed the free passage of auxiliaries through Prussian territory, encouraged by Minister v. d. Horst. Naturally, Elliot attributed this sudden change of Prussian policy to his energetic protests and reported to home about it in laughable fashion as a personal triumph. "Now, where the king viewed the political horizon as cloudy and did not feel well," reported the envoy on February 22, 1778, in a boastful letter to home, "I tried to set an objective for the negotiations with the American agents. I made it clear that I must leave Berlin if one of them was received. The result was that Lee's intended visit to Berlin has been declined (he had already been rejected 6 months earlier). The king seems now to suddenly sense the impropriety of his behavior and the danger in which he hovered of losing an ally who had earlier been the main lever of his success."

The more serious the complications of Bavaria threatened to shape, the more Frederick gave in. Elliot now suddenly believed in him more than he had earlier distrusted him. He reported home that his Prussian Majesty would never act in an acknowledging stance towards the rebels in contradiction of his great character. Schulenburg repeatedly assured him that they had absolutely rejected all rebel offers. Elliot informed Suffolk that the tools of a certain party in France had only served in the name of the king of Prussia to achieve their own aims. Frederick had always been a stranger to such plans.

It now mattered above all to probe England and demonstrate the necessity of joint dealings with Prussia by way of the Electorate of Hanover. Frederick insinuated, on the hush, that his policies against the colonies were hinged on the resolution that England would mount in the War of the Bavarian Succession. On March 28, 1778, to intimidate them even more and pull them to his side, he made the "Important Confidential" communication to the English envoy through his minister, Finckenstein, saying that the Imperial court in Vienna had hounded the king of France to recognize the independence of the colonies and to attack England's German possessions. This was already occurring without Maria Theresia having had a hand in it. The king, observed Finckenstein, would do anything to ward off an assault from England. However, since his efforts for such a noble and wholesome purpose could easily prove ineffective, he arranged, for the king of England's friendship, to inform him of impending danger which threatened his electoral possessions. Frederick hoped that appropriate measures for their defense could be agreed upon. It took all the simple-mindedness of a conceited diplomat to take these initiations as something other than a response to Kaunitz's earlier suspicions and a start-up to a new alliance with England. But Elliot reported it, most flattered by the confidence shown in him, as hard coin to Suffolk, who looked further and declared the king's statement to be an unjust and untrue claim. But since Hannover was helplessly exposed to a Prussian attack during that time, he was careful not to break with Frederick, and England stayed neutral during the War of the Bavarian Succession without committing to any duties. The English minister even declared in Potsdam that he would renew the old association with Prussia with pleasure in an even broader manner, and at the same time informed the king of the negotiations that the envoy, Harris, undertook in Saint Petersburg for the induction of an English-Russian-Prussian coalition which never actually materialized. Prussia, incidentally, was only brought in on the Empress Katarina's desire, against England's original plan.

During this time, William Lee had tracked the course of the events from Frankfurt am Main. An attempt by the French envoy, Bretruil, to include recognition of the American independence by Prussia and Russia in the Treaty of Teschen,[35] which the concerned ministers received most coldly, failed after the first initiations. After the conclusion of peace and the failure of Spain's mediation attempts between England and the United States, on August 24, 1779, Lee believed that the time had come for the king to remember his promise that he would recognize the independence of the United States as soon as France had done so. Schulenburg repeated in his reply on September 20, 1779, that Prussia had completely different concerns than the so-called naval forces. They had no right to claim any kind of direct influence in maritime law issues. It would not be wise politics to take any measures in such affairs since they could not be supported by a war fleet; thus, it remained useless. There was little objection to be had against this open explanation, dictated from a healthy policy. Lee saw that as well and answered on October 1 that he would be patient.

In a matter that was almost hopeless from the beginning, this toughness would hardly seem understandable to such calm and

35 Treaty signed by Austria and Prussia, bringing an end to the War of the Bavarian Succession.

calculating men like W. Lee and his friends, if there was not so much at stake for them in Prussia and if they had not at the same time hoped to win solid ground among the remaining continental forces, especially Holland, through their recognition on the part of the king. John Adams gave this concept the most undisguised statement on August 4, 1779, in a letter to the President. "One of the favorite plans of Frederick," he said, "consists of turning Emden into the center of a flourishing commerce. For this reason, he has a great interest in our independence, and it is to be expected that he will be one of the first to recognize it, even more so since the result of the opening of trade with us benefits Silesia. The influence exercised by the king in the united provinces is, in fact, greater than that of any other force. His near kinship with the governors and princes of Braunschweig is a further motivation for us to seek his friendship."

This point of view alone explains W. Lee's continuation of the correspondence with Schulenburg, despite the repeated negative responses. Initially, he wrote to him on May 25, 1780, again from Brussels and shared political news with him. How little he still reckoned accommodation was proven by his silence over an event that was of the greatest scope for all smaller naval forces. At the end of 1779, upon urging by the English, the Danes had extradited two prizes to England that had been brought to Bergen by American privateers, thus making the Americans even more defenseless.

Carmichael had also continued with his reports out of Madrid and occasionally slipped in the plea for recognition at last. The minister answered in polite but meaningless words as always. On the other hand, he rejected other attempts with the short remark that the king "will not get caught up in such proposals." Such as the new inquiry by Colonel Arendt and a plan of the private councilor Van der Hey who wanted to operate commerce to America under Prussian flag with Dutch capital. Schulenburg finally became tired of the never-ending and, indeed, fruitless proceedings. The last talk that he held with the king on this subject occurred at the beginning of 1781. From Brussels, William Lee had skillfully complained to the minister on December 28, 1780, that the Courier du Bas Rhin, an influential Prussian newspaper in Kleve, had recently published extremely hostile articles against Congress. He remarked that a different tone would be more suitable to better encourage harmony and good relations between both nations. At the same time, it had reported that individual Americans wanted to open trade with Emden and had inquired about the Prussian customs regulations themselves. Schulenburg sent this letter to the king on January 8, 1781, with the remark that the supposed intention of the commerce with Emden seemed to him to simply be a pretext to reconnect. Frederick answered on January 9: "Concerning your second statement, I must make known to you that we can deal with the Americans less now than usual. We must maintain a much more perfect neutrality in the matter, and you only need see consequently what hubbub the Dutch have made of it. Therefore, it is not fitting that we do anything with the Americans now. They can come to Emden, that is all well and good, but I cannot protect them because I have no navy."

Here ends the American side's official attempts to establish trade relations with Prussia during the Revolutionary War. At the beginning of December 1781, the previously-mentioned Sayre again offered the founding of a trading company in Emden that would mediate the direct trade of Prussia with the East and West

Indies. However, the king did not agree to this or any similar propositions from the enterprising English. In December 1782, Colonel Arendt once again reported to Berlin to give clarifications about American commerce but was unceremoniously refused. At the end of May 1783, the sojourning "Jew and famous artist" Jacob Philadelphia[36] made proposals in Koethen to open trade relations with the Americans, whom he had known since his youth, but they were also unfavorably decided against.

The Treaty of Teschen had barely been concluded before Frederick began to feel his old resentment against the English return. On February 8, 1780, he even gave permission for the free passage of recruits through his territory only under the condition that this would be the last time it was addressed because Germany became more depopulated by the day. However, at the next petition for the same favor, he had already forgotten this objection and granted it without any decency. Soon relations were again just as strained and hostile as before the outbreak of the War of the Bavarian Succession. England saw its most passionate and most malicious enemy in Frederick, who counteracted English influence at all corners and ends of Europe. In 1779 and 1780, he stood in the way of English politics in Saint Petersburg, where the shrewd negotiations of the Prussian envoy, Count Goertz, frustrated and partially foiled the intentions of the English envoy, Harris, multiple times. Suffolk viewed with horror this influence the king won in Copenhagen, the Hague, and even seemed to win in Paris. In the end, the English minister smelled Prussian intrigue and betrayal everywhere. Even the little pinpricks that Frederick gave Elliot acquired a much greater significance in his eyes than they,

36 Jewish-American who considered himself a scientist but was viewed as a kind of magician or occultist. He traveled the world practicing his skills and eventually was banned from Prussia after supposedly reading the king's mind.

in fact, had or should have had. "The Prussian king's hate," wrote Suffolk to Elliot on May 9, 1780, "is so irreconcilable, evoked by so little from us and is shown everywhere with such tirelessness and in so many countless forms that we can hardly expect the attitude of our court will bring forth any essential alteration in his policies. Without having even a single well-founded grievance, he acts everywhere as the bitterest enemy of England, encourages the aspirations of France, and directs all his efforts as well as a full arsenal of mockery and jest against the nation whose efforts for his favor are probably only kept alive due to its nostalgia. His Majesty behaves so aggressively against us in Russia, Holland, and everywhere. I am inclined to believe that his policies arise not only out of passion but rather out of certain secret commitments that he has undertaken with the Versailles cabinet. Unfortunately, a standing product of Count Panin's[37] political credo constitutes submissiveness towards the king of Prussia and unconditional trust in his principles, to the misfortune of England and Russia."

Towards Elliot, the king liked now more than ever to question the mere possibility of suppressing the American revolution. If bad news came, he would ask Elliot what he thought of England's prospects for a favorable conclusion of the war. He loved to excessively exaggerate the American successes. After the outbreak of English hostilities against Holland, his bitterness possibly increased against the "Islanders." On February 21, 1781, Lord Stormont, Suffolk's successor, lamented in a letter to Elliot, "We find the king of Prussia to be the most spiteful enemy of England and the most active loyal friend of France in every quarter of Europe. I wish to be informed by you about the expansion of the current alliance between the cabinets of Potsdam and Versailles as

37 Highly esteemed Russian statesman who advocated for closer ties of his monarch Catherine the Great with Frederick the Great.

well as the steps Frederick takes to secure the court of Copenhagen and to guide its policies according to his and his ministers' plans."

At that time, the king had just approached Denmark to protect the Prussian merchants with its warships against the recurrence of English acts of violence, which had recently become more common. The diplomatic proceedings towards satisfaction of this dragged out and eventually shattered. England asserted that it only captured Dutch ships sailing under Prussian flag and those that have been condemned as prizes in the English ports. The king wanted the principle that the vessel's flag be recognized, based on armed neutrality, just like the Russian aegis had towards England. Stormont refused this quite decisively and explained that since England had nothing to do with the conclusion of that agreement and had no special shipping or commerce treaty with the king of Prussia, it was only bound by the (then) principles of international law. Frederick sought help against this policy, which was thoroughly justified according to the English standpoint, through a tighter association with Denmark.

In the meantime, significant changes were being prepared in English politics. The capture of Lord Cornwallis at Yorktown on October 19, 1781, decided the independence of America. In England, the party for peace won the upper hand. The ministry of North was ousted in March 1782 and was replaced by the coalition ministry of Rockingham. It only truly held office until July 1, 1782, when its leader died.[38] Nevertheless, it made peace offerings to America and Holland and prepared the peace agreements. Its successor, the Ministry of Shelbourne, also turned to France and concluded the Treaties of Versailles on January 20, 1783, with them and the other remaining powers involved in the war.

38 Charles Watson-Wentworth, 2nd Marquess of Rockingham - died from the flu 14 weeks after being appointed to his second term as Prime Minister.

Both of these new ministries set themselves immediately towards friendlier relations with Frederick. He, full of praise for the new administrations, returned their courtesy, especially since his long-standing friendly relationship with Russia had just threatened to cool down. In place of the previous spitefulness and irritability, the desire to return to the alliance framework, which earlier had existed between the powers, stepped in on both sides. Also, the previous envoy, Elliot, made way for Sir John Stepney in the summer of 1782. The king encouraged the peace negotiations and received regular communication about their progress from the English minister. Instead of their predecessors' attempts to continue his isolation, these ministries offered everything to win him over and form an alliance in communion with Russia and the remaining Nordic powers. This was a plan that Frederick vigorously endorsed and pursued with even greater penchant since his envoy in Saint Petersburg endorsed it and deemed it practically feasible.

The certified English envoys at the foreign courts now reported from all sides about the Prussian cabinet's changed behavior and the almost friendly attitude of its policies. On June 29, 1782, the Secretary of State wrote to Sir J Harris in Saint Petersburg, "What you report regarding the conduct of the Austrian and Prussian ambassadors agrees exactly with what we have heard from other parts of Europe. I am relying on you to spare no effort to treat the latter as friendly as possible and to show them how very delighted the king of England and the current administration are about the benevolence which his Prussian majesty has shown to this country." A note designated as "Strictly Confidential and Secret" from that same minister to the newly-appointed Berlin envoy on September 20, 1782, explained in much more detail about the plans at that time. "The might of Russia," it read, "is so great that a tight alliance with them and the remaining Nordic powers should always be the goal of those, such as we, who wish to form a counterweight against the house of Bourbon. The current courteous steps are only followed for this beneficial purpose. The dearest wish of the Empress, her Maritime Code, should gladly be accepted in exchange for the return of our trust and support, and the proposal of an alliance will be made to her, even if it has been ineffective until now. All the same, our king is not discouraged and keeps in mind all of the positives of a firm and stable association with the North. The revelation of these views has had a significant effect on the king of Prussia. I can date the favorable turn in his language towards our country to the moment when it was first opened up to him. Since then, he has been treated with the greatest trust and often has been asked for his advice, which he has always given openly and honestly. His Prussian Majesty now assumes a small role in all events of England's foreign and domestic policies. I believe that a major feature of his character is his personal hatred and jealousy toward the Emperor. He is inclined to form an eventual alliance with us, Russia, and Denmark, but he is obviously against it taking place during the current war since it could easily involve him in the war. He has explained his views to his envoy here, who has informed us of them, and which I communicate to you in the deepest confidence, on different occasions since last March (the fall of the North ministry). They might serve as proof of the mutual trust which now prevails between us. I must note that what lastly concerns the council of the king of Prussia is that he prefers direct negotiation over mediation, like that offered by Katharina regarding the cession of Menorca, which was eagerly desired. He would gladly have a hand in the matter. Russia must be probed about this. The state of affairs in Saint Petersburg is now such that attempting a proposition would be fruitless. Although instructions are given for this objective, is it essential that the king of Prussia be assured that the lack of success cannot be attributed to our court. Count Görtz, his local envoy, will confirm that to him most emphatically."

Sir John Stepney reported on his first audience with the king on October 22, 1782, where he commented in detail about the political situation and the American affairs. "Thereupon," so it said in the shared report, "the king disseminated with great frankness and in clear expressions about the American war. He spoke decidedly against the withdrawal of troops and asked me about other concerns on this measure after implementation. Where could they be better needed? Regarding the independence of the colonies, His Majesty believed that since no direct benefit arises out of their direct recognition, this should be delayed until it is a necessary condition at the conclusion of the general peace. The king further noted that he was convinced that the American union could not long endure in its current form. The great expanse of the country alone would be a sufficient obstacle because a republican form of government, as is well known, has never existed in the long run where the territory has not been confined and closely connected – *concentre*[39] was his term. It would be just as absurd as if one wanted to form a democracy for the entire distance between Brest and Riga. Venice, Holland, and Switzerland allow no corollaries to be drawn since their situations and conditions are quite different from our colonies. Therefore, England should keep the United States' potential split in mind and utilize the mildest means to secure the friendly attitude of all parties. He went so far as to say that the time certainly will come when some American provinces

39 French: 'concentrated'.

would wish to again share in the advantages of the English government and to send representatives to Parliament.

Regarding the northerly settlements still in our possession, the king said one should receive them carefully and keep a watchful eye upon the local commanders-in-chief. Should they go astray, France and Spain would undoubtedly increase their claims and make peace impossible for us. He closed his remarks about America with the advice that General Carlton should proceed with caution and kindness, whereby he frequently repeated the word '*douceur.*'"[40]

Soon after these communications, peace came about. England, weakened by the American war, initially kept away from continental politics and took no part in Katharina and Joseph's actions towards the impending involvements in Turkey.[41] Of course, the United States moved completely to the background for the moment.

The result, or rather the fruitlessness of the negotiations conducted during the Revolutionary War, can be summed up in a couple of sentences. Both sides wanted to exploit and use each other without offering a tangible return. The king sought to win trading advantages but refused to risk anything at all. The Americans strove for political advantage at present but put off the future because of the counter value. From a purely commercial standpoint, they are so significantly superior to the king that he does not fully understand them: his anxious clinging to the heresies of the mercantile system, his constant fear of giving more than he could gain, his clumsy expectation that the first attempt must amount to a double and triple profit, and his petty view of overseas enterprises. All these weaknesses and concerns would

40 French: 'sweetness'.

41 Referring to the Russo-Turkish War and Austro-Turkish War.

hardly be believable if they were not spelled out in his own words. In the end, the whole negotiations shrunk down to a little business on a couple of shiploads in the interest of Prussian tobacco production. To the poor Prussia of that time, 200,000 Thalers amounted to a great and risky transaction! Admittedly, the benefits that the Americans offered were of a very questionable nature. However, the United States' internal ailments were not known to the poorly-informed king and his ministers, so those benefits were considered accurate in their eyes. However, he was quite right politically if he did not accept the American proposals. Compared to England, he was too weak to have a rift with them or to even allow humiliations from the English fleet. The Americans themselves were mistaken in all of their political preconditions and were, therefore, harshly disappointed. The king had adopted their propositions and communications only as a map, which he could possibly play off for his own interests. But the opportunity did not arise, so the map stayed in his hand.

The Prussian-American Treaty of Amity and Commerce

The Treaty of Paris[42] was finally concluded on September 3, 1783, after a war lasting more than eight years. The United States saw its independence recognized by all of Europe from then on. But they had barely saved the survival and freedom of their existence during the great struggle and still had to prove their viability and political entitlement. Poor and almost helpless, without internal support or coherence, at best like a shared debt. A loose confederation that threatened to fall apart again at any moment. Viewed with disdain by the great naval powers, yet not even with suspicion, and even doubting if it would succeed in maintaining its independence given the internal difficulties which accumulated with every passing day, the new free state looked to increase its trade and its resources by utilizing

42 Treaty that officially ended the Revolutionary War and defined the boundaries separating the British territories of North America and the United States.

foreign friends and alliances. Thus, it was not Europe that imposed its friendship on the Congress; it was the young republic that was just coming into life, which promoted its friendly and commercial relations to the mature political communities.

There was nothing humiliating about this completely natural relationship, as the United States proudly and confidently claimed its appropriate position in the international community. The men who guided their nation's destiny in that critical period, such as Franklin, Adams, Jefferson, Jay, Duane, Morris, and many others, felt their personal responsibility before the world and their people. Consequently, they grasped the notion for which they had committed their lives from the victory—the notion of the entitlement and existence of their national independence. Instead of bowing and flattering themselves into the dominant powers' circle, they considered themselves of equal ranking with Europe's great nations from the first instant of their political presence and acted accordingly. As if in anticipation of their bright future, they demanded the recognition of certain international law principles which envisaged freedom at sea and eventually helped initiate an era-making reform of maritime law as the price for their friendship.

This bold and reforming position was undoubtedly made easier for them at the beginning since the most exaggerated imaginations of the profits of American commerce were had in Europe in those days. Every maritime and trading power, no matter how small, believed to be able to draw a share for themselves, hence lent an attentive ear to the American friendship and commercial propositions. Franklin and Adams could write home that all of Europe wished to establish trade relations and conclude agreements with them.

But this favorable atmosphere did not last long. Soon after completion of the peace, they re-established the old commercial dealings with England, just as they had been in colonial times. The American people had not stopped thinking, speaking, and living as English. Their habits, desires, and pleasures were almost exclusively English. Therefore, the trade traffic between both countries expanded daily all the more. On the one hand, the trade restrictions of the mightiest competitor, France, did not allow an exchange that was free and advantageous for both sides. On the other hand, commerce was only possible with English houses, and the willingly-granted large credit from them had created an English monopoly.

Before this knowledge had broken into other circles, Congress decided on May 7, 1784, to draw benefit from the advantageous atmosphere of the foreign countries. They commissioned three specially appointed commissioners for this purpose, the envoys Adams, Franklin, and Jefferson. Not only to finalize friendship and trade agreements with distinguished states well-known to them, such as the small German states, Prussia, Denmark, Portugal, Spain, the Papal States, and Tuscany; but rather to also extend these to Russia, England, Sardinia, Saxony, Hamburg, Genoa, Venice, the North African robber states if possible, and to amend the already-completed agreements with France, Holland, and Sweden once and for all on the basis of instructions newly issued to them. These instructions contained the same liberal principles in nine different paragraphs, which later found their language in the treaty completed with Prussia. Originating from the assumption and condition that the United States, in accordance with the provisions of the Federal Constitution, is a united and single nation – which they became five years later – in the first section, they requested for each of the contracting parties the right to bring their products, wares, and brands into the port of the other in their own ships, to get the products of the other from there and to only pay the same customs duties paid by the most favored nations in both cases. In the second section, they required direct commerce for the United States in the colonies of those nations that had colonies in America or, if that could not be attained, a direct transport with specific ports within the colony's territory. If this proviso also should not be taken, they claimed the concession that the United States and such colonies may import and export their mutual wares directly in their own ships. The fourth section suggests, although it is not demanded as an indispensable condition, that in the case of a war, the merchants of a war belligerent may stay in the country of the other for nine months to put their affairs in order.

Furthermore, that all peaceful citizens who dwell on the flat land or in unfortified cities and work for the better of mankind, especially farmers, craftsmen, and artists, as well as merchants who mediate the exchange of products, should not be troubled nor bothered by enemies. What is taken from them must be paid for in cash. None of the contracting parties may issue letters of marque[43] to interrupt the commerce of the enemy or to destroy their ships. In the event of war, the goods that are designated as contraband, such as weapons, munitions, etc., that are found on the ships of one war belligerent on their way to the enemy of the other are not to be counted as contraband, so they can not be confiscated and lost to private individuals. Meanwhile, it shall be legal to hold such ships for as long as the captor sees fit, to avoid

43 A license issued by a government to an individual that authorized them to attack and capture enemy vessels and cargo; known as 'caper letter' in German.

inconvenience or harm for themselves, but shall compensate the loss caused by this means and pay for the goods used by them. However, if the contracting state wants to remain defiant of the contraband's confiscation, in that case, the concerned ship shall be made free through its relinquishment so that it need not be brought into a port, but instead can peacefully resume its journey.

The sixth section specified, almost verbatim to the set principles of armed neutrality, that all wares which are not contraband and are found on neutral ships will be spared and declared to be present upon the blockade of a port if the attacking force has taken such a position that the ships which want to enter into the threatened port would be exposed to obvious danger by attempting to do so. The seventh and last section allowed the heirs of foreigners who died in the United States to realize the testator's estate within the required time.

It is easy to find the weaknesses in these directives. Nevertheless, their extreme importance cannot be denied. Sound constitutional principles and an austere perception of the actual living conditions stand next to sentimental phrases and blurry future plans. A cosmopolitan yearning for peace, which lacks any substrate of power, appeals to the monopoly that is found to be extremely sound in the present conditions and tries to wrest away control by establishing the hybrid situation of a peaceful war, as if politics were not a battle of rival interests and principles. This mixture of unclear fantasies and entitled demands constitutes one of the characteristic features of that time, running blind against the existing and emerging history, and only raves about the best to be created from the new worlds. It imagines having reached the height of human progress with radical utopias. This time is only clear on one point; its appreciation of the bad past. However, it must be entrusted to the future to reveal the healthy core from the chaos of their demands and axioms.

To dissect the directives in their individual components, there stands, first of all, the demand for the repeal of the trade monopoly. It stands in direct opposition to the previous commercial policies of England, France, and Spain. Thus, the powers who controlled the seas naturally wanted to assert their domination, so they did not have any reason in the least to sacrifice their profit and position to an abstract legal principle. The United States, due to its maritime insignificance at the time, was not in a position to concede any privileges to others in exchange for the privileges granted to them. Without a doubt, an extraordinary beneficial reform would have been achieved in the then trading system with the adoption of their demands. But the naval powers treated the transatlantic Republic's suggestions with the same compassionate disdain as a rich baron looks down on a poor devil who suggests a sharing of his fortune in the name of humanity because of his poverty and powerlessness. But the fourth section demands something absolutely impossible in that it wants the farmers, craftsmen, and merchants to be excluded from the events of war. As if its horrors were thereby mitigated, as if they would not fall with double weight on the other members of the nation in the event of the acceptance of this clause! Especially in a Republic where each citizen should be the defender of his fatherland, to expect that certain classes be exempted from the troubles of war and pursue their occupations to enrich themselves during nationwide ruin so that they don't raise the price of certain life necessities and thus doubly bleed the other citizens! Instead of cutting short and decreasing hostile encounters, such a policy would only extend and multiply them. There is a purely mercantile conception of war that has not yet been overcome in the United States, even today. The miserable recruiting system that arguably hires soldiers but knows no fatherland defender, leaves the common national interests and honor out of the game as unjustified factors, and calculates national fortune. War is often fortunate or misfortune for a nation according to dollars and cents.

Were these suggestions dictated by sentimentality or commercial calculation? Apparently, a little bit of both. But at the bottom of the soul of the instructing Congress, the commercial selfishness prevailed, and sentimentality only served them as a fig leaf,[44] at least according to the resolution composed a half year earlier. The United States had been immediately asked to join the armed neutrality[45] after the conclusion of the armistice and had hurried to instruct their agents in Europe in an affirmative sense, but found upon closer consideration that they could easily be involved in European disputes and naval wars through such an accession without being able to count on the help of the remaining neutrals, as the example of Holland had proven. Therefore, they withdrew their commitment on October 19, 1783, in the following words, "Since the acquisition of aid for our independence constitutes the main subject matter of the instructions of our minister for the armed nationality, you will find that we no longer need this aid as a result of the recently entered into treaties for the restoration of peace. Although Congress upholds the principles of that agreement since it was closed on the liberal foundation of the assertion

44 A reference to the fig leaves that Adam and Eve used to cover up their nudity after eating the forbidden fruit; a metaphor used to signify a flimsy excuse for or the covering up of something shameful or sinister.

45 The state of neutrals staying armed to defend themselves against incursions from war waging parties, with the first League of Armed Neutrality being established in 1780 to protect neutral shipping in the War of Independence and later formed the basis for international law.

of neutral rights, under the current conditions, they are not willing to become a member of a federation that could complicate the interests of the United States with the policies of Europe in the near future. Hence, if the proceedings are not already so far advanced, it is the wish of Congress to make our dishonorable withdrawal and send instruction to all our envoys in Europe that they seize no further measures for the purpose of the accession of the United States to the armed neutrality."

Thus, they wanted nothing other than to be a commercial nation and to conclude their alliances merely based on trading benefits offered to them. They even imagined that they could avoid every political intricacy through their neutrality and did not have to learn, which they did to their detriment thirty years later via a war forced upon them,[46] that their own intentions alone were not authoritative in such issues; instead, the neighbors also had a decisive say. But be that as it may, these instructions included a couple of provisions that stood as lighthouses of a better future and assigned the United States, right from the beginning of their history, to a proud position among the maritime powers, despite all reprimanded weaknesses and deficiencies. It is these great principles that proclaimed the freedom of the seas and have been bravely and energetically championed up to the present day. It is these doctrines of the neutrals' rights, of the freedom of property on neutral ships, of the nature of contraband, and of the requirements of the validity of blockade that they had first decidedly established. These have turned out to be for the common good of almost all nations since the Treaty of Paris of 1856 and have already partially found their place in modern international law despite all initial contradictions. As the United States' independence initiated and announced the story of the modern era, so

46 War of 1812.

the instructions from May 7, 1784, discarded the medieval jungle-law[47] of the sea. Being the first most damaging impact on the mischief of the pirate characters; they described the beginning of a new era of peaceful international transport at sea. Indeed, armed neutrality, in particular, had already been expressed in a similar sense in earlier agreements. While those requirements deliberately erected by the United States were only contained partially as ancillary provisions and random details, the federation, from February 28, 1780, owed its emergence more as a diplomatic intrigue and to the dexterity of Panin.[48] In short, by chance, and soon dissolved again after he had formulated its famous principles. However, the United States is due the immortal merit for elevating these principles to their foreign policy platform, thereby humanizing international law on the sea a little, even if it still took almost two generations until these principles secured the universal recognition of the civilized world. So strong is their power and their influence that they have outlasted the setbacks within. Even a minster like Marcy, whose term of office denotes the pinnacle of internal degradation and weakness, acquired the reputation of a liberal statesman in the eyes of Europe due to his taking up the theoretical executive position in maritime law issues in 1856, albeit with injustice.

Incidentally, the American commissioners, despite all of their zealous efforts, failed to win a single one of the states named to them for a trade agreement and the new international law doctrines, with the sole exception of Prussia. These apparently went too far for them. That is easy to comprehend with the great maritime powers; they simply did not want to lose their domination

47 Referring to the 'law of the jungle,' i.e., only the strong survive, no laws or morals, etc.

48 Referring to the First League of Armed Neutrality.

over the sea without any compensation. However, the smaller powers dared not break with the old ways without the example of the greater powers, or, on the other hand, they might have convinced themselves that the trade traffic with the United States would not yield the expected profits in the beginning.

For the present examination we only consider Prussia. The Prussian treaty is actually the fourth in the sequence of agreements that the United States entered into with European powers and the first of those after the peace. During the war, only two states had completed friendship and trade agreements with Congress. France entered into the first to supplement their alliance on February 6, 1778, and then Holland, the second, on October 8, 1782, who found themselves at war with England at that time and consequently had nothing to lose. Sweden followed next on April 3, 1783, in the period between the armistice and final peace. The Swedish agreement distinguishes itself from its predecessors. It committed to the principles of armed neutrality, as it is well known that one of its most ardent supporters was Gustav III. Also, Hamburg, on March 29, 1783, like a good merchant, sought to make use of the beneficial economic situation after the peace and extolled the most beneficial goods that the US could obtain from them, including German fabric, Westphalian and Silesian linen, paper, glass, wine, and all types of East Indies and Chinese goods in addition to its friendship and admiration for the transatlantic free state. Congress gave a courteous response to the carrier of this agreeable writing, Johann Abraham de Boor, on Nov 1, 1783, but found no occasion to undertake a special alliance with Hamburg.

As the instructions discussed above were issued, Prussia and the United States' first negotiations were already hovering. In the last years of the American war, the king had never wholly lost sight of establishing trade relations with the young Republic. Even during the peace negotiations, he provided his Paris envoy, Baron v d Goltz, with the necessary instructions. On July 22, 1783, Franklin wrote home that Prussia also wished to engage in trade with America and that its envoy, if he could directly put forward any agreement, had handed him a list of items with the request that they be submitted to the attention of American merchants.[49] Goltz first made a formal proposition towards the end of 1783. On November 17, the king had ordered him to finally contact the American agents or envoys in Paris directly, and in particular, to ascertain what could be done for Prussian woolen and linen goods in America and if tobacco and rice could be obtained in exchange. "If that can be done," closed the king, "you will prove to me a great service because a more direct trade is worth more than one obtained second-hand." On December 2, Goltz excused his apparent idleness, reporting that Franklin still had not received an answer regarding the list of Prussian merchandise handed over to him in the summer and sent to America.

Meanwhile, he had displayed great delight over the prospects introduced to him of a direct trade connection with Prussia. On February 15, 1784, the next feedback from the envoys occurred. However, they were still not in a position to give the impatient king adequate information.

"Mr. Franklin," he wrote, "is still in the country and, through his grandson, has let me say that he regrets to still be unable to clearly answer me about bringing the trade between the states of Your Majesty and the Americans into being. Still, the lists provided by me have been communicated to the trading cities. He is convinced that they will use them for various speculations for our

49 The Works of Benjamin Franklin, Vol. IX, 539-540.

mutual benefit. On my question of why the administration does not take a bigger role in the plans, the young Franklin replied that the single reason is that there is a complete standstill of all foreign affairs. This was brought about as much through the dismissal submitted by the foreign minister as through the internal movements that demand Congress's complete attention. His grandfather, who three months ago had come for his recall, has still not even received a reply from Congress" (which, by the way, was also not possible).

Even before this letter was written, the impatient king had turned to his envoy in the Hague, Mr. von Thulemeyer,[50] and dictated to him a handwritten postscript from February 9. "Try to speak with a certain Adams, who was sent to Holland on behalf of the Americans, and find out whether there are any means or ways to set us in agreement with those people for the sale of our linen and the purchase of their Virginian tobacco." Thulemeyer had always reported in short notes to the king about American dealings in Holland and even reported on January 30 that John Adams had come to Amsterdam to take care of the final formalities of the American-Dutch treaty from October 8, 1782. He now replied promptly on February 17, "I will, according to the command of His Majesty, get in touch with Mr. Adams and question him about the means as to how a reciprocal trade can be initiated for Virginian tobacco and Silesian linen between the earlier English colonies and the states of the Prussian monarchy. I have already earlier used the mediation of an American chargé d'affaires

50 Friedrich Wilhelm von Thulemeyer, who would become Justice Minister in 1788.

(Dumas)[51] to allow the proposals of a Silesian manufacturer reach Philadelphia through him. It seems that the lack of cash money in American is now made very noticeable."

On February 20, Thulemeyer sent the king a comprehensive report. Its contents match almost verbatim Adams' letter following below from March 9, 1784, to Congress. Through this report, Frederick was prompted to commission Thulemeyer with the further negotiations and eventual conclusion of an agreement.

Thulemeyer belonged to a proven and long-standing Westphalian bureaucratic family. The father, Heinrich Wilhelm, came from Minden, was ennobled in 1728 by Frederick Wilhelm I, and appointed as a state and cabinet minister. The son, Frederick Wilhelm, was born in 1735 in Berlin and trained in the "nursery of the department for foreign affairs." He was already appointed in 1763 as an envoy in the Hague, a position in which he remained for a full 24 years. Promoted to the state and justice minister in 1793, he held this position until the catastrophe of the year 1806. After its occurrence, he withdrew himself from the office. Thulemeyer died in 1807 and left behind the reputation, equally of a proficient, experienced official and as a patriotic and highly educated man.

Of John Adams, suffice it to note that he would become Washington's successor as president of the United States. He was of an austere, robust nature, a calm observer, a great diplomat, and one of his nation's most worthy representatives in foreign countries. In his political views, in contrast to his later colleagues, Franklin and Jefferson, Adams inclined more on the real perceptions of English laws, which he had thoroughly studied and

---

51 Charles Dumas was also employed as a secret agent in Europe and had even devised a code for the secret correspondence between the Continental Congress and its agents in Europe.

practiced. The English constitution stood higher in his view than all that the French of that time called philosophy. While these theories were drawn up and reasoned, Adams went back to experience and history and sought to learn from them. He did not conceal the insignificance of the United States at that time for a moment. Thus, he also properly dignified his own delicate position and behaved in England as in Holland with remarkable tact and skill.

Incidentally, both men already stood on good terms with each other before the opening of negotiations, and Thulemeyer had proven to be especially useful to Adams, even on his first appearance in the diplomatic circles of the Dutch residence. The American envoy had already been received by Holland as such, at a time when American independence was still not yet recognized by the remaining European powers. Thus, he was valid in the eyes of his new colleagues only as a rebel agent. As Adams had paid his inaugural visit to them, significant concerns were raised among the diplomats whether or not they were allowed to respond. Indeed, one was near thereon to completely ignore him or, as the English expression reads, 'to show the cold shoulder.' Finally, Thulemeyer found a way out of the ridiculous quandary and proposed that Adams should make a second visit but render his card only with his name, without the addition of any title or official position. This suggestion was found acceptable; the diplomats reciprocated the visit correspondingly with the devising of a simple visiting card, and Adams was accepted as a gentleman, if not as an envoy, among the diplomats.[52] These proceedings had taken place in the spring of 1782. Since then, the relations between both the American and the Prussian envoys had always been friendly. "The minister from Prussia, Mr. von Thulemeyer," wrote Adams on September 4,

52 St. P. O. Prussia, Vol.124, No.8.

1782, to the state secretary Livingston, "is very polite towards me and attacks me, as he puts it, in the English language. Since we are both great horsemen, he wishes to ride out together with me. He speaks unreserved with me about astronomy and scientific matters, but this class of people is very restrained in political things. They must always wait for their instructions."

About one and a half years later, Thulemeyer and Adams entered into businesslike dealings with each other. The former opened the negotiations, as can be seen from the above-communicated orders. "On the 18th of February," wrote Adams on March 9, 1784, to the Congress, "Mr. von Thulemeyer did me the honor of a visit. But as he found I had company he soon took his leave again. As I accompanied him to the stairs, he said to me that he has a proposition to make to me on the behalf of the king and desires to know when he might call again. The next day at 11 o'clock he came back, instead of letting me reciprocate his visit, and said the king, who graced him with a personal correspondence, is familiar with my character and has instructed him to visit me and to tell me that since his subjects need our tobacco and other articles while we need Silesian linen together with some other Prussian goods, His Majesty believes that an arrangement between Prussia and the United States would be advantageous for both parties. On Thulemeyer's questioning towards my opinion of the matter I replied that I feel very flattered from the honor shown to me by His Majesty, however I have no authority to negotiate the matter officially or to enter into discussions thereover at all. That although Congress has authorized its ministers at the latest peace negotiations to start up such negotiations, I can only act in fellowship with Mr.'s Franklin and Jay who are situated in Paris, but I thought I could answer for the good dispositions of those gentlemen as well as my own for the forming of an arrangement between the two power which might be beneficial for both, and that I would write to those ministers about the initiations made by me. Thulemeyer asked me to do that and added that he will write with the first post to the king and inform him of my answer and at the same time inquire whether he still has anything in particular to propose. On the next day I wrote to Paris and last Saturday received a letter from Dr Franklin and Mr Jay in which they both expressed their conviction that the friendly attitude of his Prussian majesty will give the Congress great pleasure. The respect with which the reputation of that great ruler has impressed the United States has early induced them to consider his friendship as a highly desirable object, and we are happy in being authorized to assure His Majesty that they will most cheerfully enter into such a commercial treaty with him, as being founded on principles of reciprocity may be productive of equal benefit to both countries. Although we have no commission to conclude such a treaty, our instructions from Congress enable us to join with the Prussian minister in preparing a draft of such a treaty which upon its submission to Congress they would issue formal authority to conclude the treaty and give us pointed instructions on the subject and much time might be thereby saved. If you are of this opinion and His Majesty should be pleased to approve such a measure, we think the articles may be discussed between you and Baron von Thulemeyer in the first instance on grounds of the principles which govern the treaties you have mentioned, both of which have already been approved and ratified with Holland and Sweden. That being done, we might confer with each other and write a joint letter to Congress on the subject.

Yesterday upon meeting the Baron (Thulemeyer) at court on

the occasion of Prince of Orange's birthday, he told me that he had received another letter from the king and in the evening would call on me for an audience. He did that and informed me that the king was gathering all necessary papers and would soon send them to him with his further propositions to be made to me. I showed him my letter from Paris, with which he was highly pleased. Thulemeyer added that the king had directed him to mention rice and indigo as articles in demand in Emden and Stettin and that a significant quantity of Virginian tobacco had been purchased in this year in those ports for the markets in the Baltic Sea, while the excellent Saxon porcelain might be a desirable article for the Americans. I take the liberty of submitting to Congress whether the model of the treaties concluded with Holland or Sweden may not serve as the best model for one to be completed with Prussia, and whether it is advisable to send a fully authorized power to their ministers to conclude this business."

Thulemeyer reported to the king on February 20, 1784, about the satisfactory impression of his first meeting with Adams and anticipated few difficulties for a treaty since the principles of his government stressed by the American envoy are so simple and just, that they would unquestionably have the approval of the king. He suggested the treaty which the United States had concluded with Sweden as the model for the one to be agreed with Prussia. Initially, Frederick said (in a cabinet order to Schulenburg from March 7, 1784), "The treatise which the Swedes have established with the Americans does not entirely fit our circumstances, particularly due to our linen and fabric which we transport to America and which the Swedes don't have. Also, many things are contained in the Swedish treatise that pertain to fleets. That is fine for Sweden because they have fleets, but not for us, since we have no such fleets. I want to instruct you to make a rough draft of a treatise for us once you have looked over the Swedish treaty." Finckenstein, on the other hand, remarked that, "even if not all articles of the Swedish trade treaty fit with ours because we have no fleet, we maintain that most of them will still be applicable and that we don't have to tie our hands for the future." Schulenburg just as emphatically eliminated the king's initial plan that Amsterdam should be the intermediary place for the Prussian and American trade.

"I believe," he wrote on April 3, 1784, to the foreign minister, "the mistake that Amsterdam would be the storehouse of this commerce partly lies in the fact that the king's dominion is just not ported for the purpose of our ships traveling to North America. But mainly because His Majesty worries that the Americans will not be able to balance their accounts with cash money since the goods they take from us will amount to far more than what we receive from them. This is why His Majesty has already expressed to me that the Dutch step into the middle and buy the Americans' remaining wares that we do not need to obtain our cash account balance. But this is based on whether the Americans even come into our ports. I believe it will be for the best if Mr. von Thulemeyer completely drops this idea concerning Amsterdam and just focuses on the project approved by His Majesty regarding the commerce treaty wherein the Americans are expressly assured of the trade advantages in the event that they come into our ports."

Just as on the earlier point, the king later yielded on this latter point. Thulemeyer could already, on March 14, 1784, agree to utilize the closed treaty with Sweden as the basis for the Prussian one and requested a copy of the former. On the 25th of the same month, he gave Adams a list of goods to introduce to Prussia and to receive from Prussia, with profits. Among the former, he mentioned Virginian tobacco, rice, indigo, and whale oil. Among the latter, he confined himself to listing Silesian linen, of which he lists various sorts according to specifications of the manufacturer, Johann Gottfried Link in Hirschberg; Russian hemp; Berlin porcelain, (which he indicated was cheaper and finer than that of Saxony); ironware from the County of the Mark,[53] which, up to now, had gone to America via England; and cloth and woolen goods of all types. On April 9, Thulemeyer submitted to Adams the draft of a treaty that was compiled by Schulenburg and conveyed to him by the king. Adams then immediately sent a copy to Franklin in Paris and, on April 10, to Congress.

This Prussian draft consisted of 27 articles and had hardly retained more than that in its final editorship, while nearly every individual paragraph had been significantly altered and, often, even in a sense that was the absolute opposite of the originals. The king's real purpose with the closure of this treaty was made clear from reading its third article. He wanted nothing other than to win new markets to sell the most important Prussian staple products and, above all, to exchange them for American tobacco, rice, and indigo. He hoped to bypass the English middleman in this manner and believed to be able to establish and direct the new union from above like any other government measure. But he had overlooked the fact that commerce has its own laws and channels and that the creation and application of capital cannot be achieved through cabinet orders. For this reason, the later agreed-to treaty was as good as a dead letter.[54] By way of its greater and more liquid

53 Located in modern-day North Rhine-Westphalia, a part of Prussia from 1701 to 1807 and again from 1813.

54 An expression used to describe when something is still valid but is inapplicable, such as an outdated law. Basically, the later treaty was irrelevant.

capital and the better connections resulting from this, England maintained its mediating position between America and Europe as before. Prussia and the United States of that time were still too lacking in both to be able to bypass or dispense with England.

After the first article stated the firm and unbreakable friendship between both powers and the second article granted each of them the same preferential treatment as granted to other nations, the third article of the Prussian draft read thus: "The principal end of this treaty being to establish a reciprocal commerce between the subjects of both states and to procure a secure and easy path for the exchange of their products for them by that means, the two contracting parties come to agree that the Prussian wares, especially Silesian and Westphalian linen, cloth and woolen fabrics shall pay no different or higher tariffs in the United States of America than those paid by the most favored nations on entry and exportation. In the same manner, the American staple products such as Virginian tobacco, rice, indigo, furs, etc. are only subject to the duties paid by the most favored nations upon their import into Prussian ports." The fourth article retained the right to prohibit the import or export of goods on the grounds of state welfare for the contracting parties. The fifth article restricted the rights of visitation and searching of goods to the time before the loading of the cargo onto ships. It specifies the form and manner of the seizure of prohibited goods on shore. The sixth article granted nationals of both countries the rights, privileges and freedoms of the most favored nations. The seventh article approved unconditional freedoms of religion and conscience for the inhabitants of each country while in the other. The eighth specified the testamentary and intestate-succession of the nationals of both countries in the movable assets of a relative who died in the other while, according to the model of the Swedish treaty, the real estate property was passed on with silence and forbade any circulation of a state tax on the answerable property. Still, the king of Prussia reserved the right to pass laws against emigration and to execute those already enacted against it. The ninth article recognized the tenet, "Free ship, Free Goods,"[55] and the tenth through twelfth articles specified the notion of contraband. All artillery, muskets, sabers, swords, mortars, munitions, sulfur, bullets, horses and saddles, and any weapons or war tools at all which may be of service or use to the troops apply as such. On the other hand, cloth, linen, wool, cotton, garments, silk, silver, copper, tin, lead, iron, coal, grain, foodstuffs of all sorts, flax, sailcloth, and everything that pertains to the construction and to the repair of ships shall not be counted as contraband. The thirteenth article decreed that if one of the parties is involved in a war, the ships of the other should be provided with the required ships' papers and passes, as well as with certificates that describe their cargo so that the verification that they carry no contraband or forbidden goods can be conducted immediately. According to article fourteen, they must present these papers upon demand. Article fifteen stipulated that if they have contraband on board that is destined for an enemy harbor, neither the hatches nor the crates may be broken until the cargo is taken ashore in the presence of an officer appointed to the task and the opening is performed by him. But even then, a procedural method must take place, and the relevant goods may only be confiscated after judgment while the remaining cargo stays free, and the ship may not be confiscated as a lawful prize. But if the mustered ship's contraband is handed over, the ship which

55 Free ship, meaning neutral ship. Thus, any goods excluding contraband, even enemy goods, were protected from attack and seizure when under neutral flag.

had carried it can pursue its course unmolested to the place of its destination. On the other hand, if a ship has been taken under the pretext that it has contraband on board, its proprietor can claim compensation for all holdups and delays if this pretext is not proven. The sixteenth article established the tenet: "Unfree ship, unfree goods,"[56] and stated that these goods shall be handed over to the owner only if they had been loaded before or no more than nine months after the declaration of war. The seventeenth article specified that the commanding officers of the ships of one party shall inflict no harm to the state or the subjects of the other contracting party and shall be personally and objectively liable for any damage done if found guilty. The eighteenth article decreed that privateers shall provide a guarantee that they will do no harm to the subjects of the other before they receive their orders from one of the counter-parties and that if they still do it, their appointment will be forfeited. According to article nineteen, if one of the contracting parties wages war but the other stays neutral, and if the merchant ship of the neutral is taken by enemies of the warring side and later is retaken by a privateer of the latter, this ship shall be brought into the harbor of one of the treaty-concluding powers and the concerned proprietor shall be reimbursed as soon as he has proven his claim. Furthermore, no embargo shall be permitted on the goods or ships of the other power, nor may they be withheld under any pretext at all if one power declares an embargo. Even less so may the subjects of one contingent take by force anything that belongs to the subjects of the other without permission of the owner. Of course, exempt from the last provision are the arrest orders and seizures ordered by the concerned justice courts. The twentieth article regulated the procedures to

56 Unfree ship, meaning enemy ship. Thus, any neutral goods under enemy flag can be subjected to confiscation.

be observed regarding prizes and recaptures in the event of a war against a common enemy. This is recorded verbatim as article 21 in the final treaty with the inclusion of a small, later addition. The 21st article of the draft determined that the ships of one power may bring their prizes taken from the enemy into the ports of the other power that remain open to friendly nations in wartime and that this prize may be neither halted nor confiscated, nor be subjected to the dictum of the concerned port officials about their legality. Instead, they may travel unencumbered from there to the ports to which the captain who captured them is obligated to bring them by virtue of his appointment, which is to be shown upon request. Articles 22 and 23 obligated the members of one state to provide assistance to the members of the other in the event of a shipwreck, to pledge support and friendship to asylum seekers, and to dismiss the bearing of the barbaric beach law.[57] Articles 24 and 25 concerned the easements and amenities of maritime policing. Article 26 conceded to each of the contingents the right to employ consuls and trade agents in the port of the other, and article 27 set the ratification period at eight months from the day of the signing, while a separate article restricted the duration of the treaty to fifteen years.

John Adams suggested only three essential modifications or rather additions to this treaty draft. The first concerned more exact and specific writing of the seventh article, which dealt with the religious and conscience freedoms because the guarantees of freedom of beliefs and conscience were not necessarily enough for him. The next modification referred to the fifteenth article, where

57 According to traditional beach law, shipwreck salvage was a finders-keepers game. However, this often descended to beach piracy, with a total disregard for the survivor's lives, sometimes resulting in the murder of survivors so as to claim the spoils of the shipwreck.

instead of the opening of ships (for the purpose of the discovery of contraband), he requested that an inventory be made. Congress declared themselves agreed with him on both points. The last of Adams' suggestions was a change to the wording of the 21st article because the treaty that had already been completed with the king of France in 1778 determined (in article 17) that the warships or privateers which had taken French or American prizes should only be granted refuge in the ports of either country as long as storm or perils at sea had forced them to come in. Therefore, Congress also restricted the 21st article to Adams' proposition in this sense,[58] since what mattered most for them was to give no reason for anyone to complain to the king of France and to set the old treaty in conformity with the new.

On May 22, 1784, the king declared himself agreed with all the American alterations except the last one. The objections that he made against the new version of the 21st article remained an open issue between both contracting powers until the end. Frederick would have most preferred to see the whole article left out of the treaty, "since we," as he put it, "do not make piracy."

These negotiations took place over the summer of 1784. Meanwhile, the instructions from May 7 arrived in the hands of the three representatives – Adams, Franklin, and Jefferson. They then met in Paris at the end of August and, in a collectively signed note dated 'Passy, Paris September 9, 1784,' informed Mr von Thulemeyer of their appointments, and at the same time declared their readiness to perfect and conclude the friendship and commerce treaty that Adams had already started with him as soon as he received full authority for this purpose. Thulemeyer replied on October 8 and enclosed the authorization that had been issued to

58 The Diplomatic Correspondence of the American Revolution, Vol. I, 459-463.

him on September 30, 1784, by the king.

The representatives sent a new counter-draft of the treaty to Thulemeyer on November 10, 1784, in response to this letter and gave impetus for this move in the following way: "Due to new instructions received from our sovereign, the Congress, we propose to you certain new articles for all our treaties to be completed with European powers, which if agreed to would render some of those heretofore in use unnecessary. Judging that some change in the order, by bringing together what relates to the same subject would render the whole more clear, we have prepared a new draft for the project adding the new articles, and send it herewith for your consideration. Those new articles are the 13th and 23rd. The first of them speaks for itself, because it is absolutely necessary to prevent the difficulties and misunderstandings which constantly arise in time of war with regard to merchandise called contraband. In support of the other we offer a few reasons contained in a separate paper to which we shall only add here that the article be in favor of humanity by softening and diminishing the calamities of war. We think it will be honorable for the first powers to agree to it and more particularly so for His Majesty the king of Prussia, especially if the king whose subjects are known to be so well defended through his power and his abilities, as to make the stipulation of any favor for them during war unnecessary, should be the foremost in setting the example of agreeing to such an article. The part too which engages not to commission privateers nor make prizes of merchant ships we think will show the disinterestedness of the United States, since their situation is suited to prey with ease of the rich commerce of Europe and the West Indies which must pass before their doors, while their own consisting in shipbuilding lumber and provisions is of so little value that the loss in that kind of war would be vastly inferior to the profit. This was demonstrated in their late war with England, whose mighty fleets were insufficient to protect the English trade from the depredations of a people who were just as able and expert sailors as themselves."

The special memorandum (article 4 of the instructions from May 4, 1784) about the new articles is interesting and the unabridged transmission worthwhile. Not so much because they stand in contradiction to all later official demonstrations of the ruling circle, but because they come from Franklin, whose argumentation and style, which are based on the French *Encyclopedists,*[59] are unmistakably expressed therein. The reform called for was one of Franklin's favorite ideas, which he had unsuccessfully sought to incorporate into the 1783 peace treaty with England. Jared Sparks, the biographer of Benjamin Franklin and publisher of his works, explained this memorandum specifically for a composition of the great Quaker, and prints it as such.

"According to the original international law," it says, "war and eradication were the penalty for an injustice. But it became gradually more humane and sat slavery in the place of death; it then took a step further and replaced them as prisoners instead of making them slaves. It went further still and recognized private property in the conquered countries while contenting themselves with political ruler-ship. Why should this international law now not be capable of further improvements? It has needed entire centuries for each of its advances. But since knowledge grows more mightily in recent times, why should this progress not accelerate, why should the international law of future ages not be determined,

59 Members of a French writers' society that contributed to the *Encyclopédie* and championed the ideas of the Enlightenment, such as secular thought, rationality, tolerance, etc.

so that in any later outbreak of war, the following class of people remain undisturbed and enjoy the protection from both sides and practice their occupations in peace and security? Namely: 1. cultivators of the soil, because they work for the upkeep of humanity; 2. Fisherman, on the same grounds; 3. Merchants in unarmed ships, because they serve different nations through the mediation and exchange of the requirements and amenities of life; 4. Artists and craftsmen who live and work in open cities. It is hardly necessary to add that the hospitals of the enemies remain unmolested; they should, on the contrary, be protected. Overall, the interest of mankind demands that the occasions of war and the instigation for it be reduced, if possible. If robbery stops, so the main appeal for war is also canceled, and the peace will then last longer, indeed perhaps always. The practice of robbing merchants on the high seas is a remnant of the old piracy, and although it may be lucrative here and there for individual persons, it is certainly far from being beneficial for those involved or the nations that allow it. At the beginning of a war, a couple of richly-loaded and incautious ships will be surprised and taken. This prompts the first adventurers to equip more armed ships, then others do the same. Meanwhile, the enemy simultaneously becomes more cautious and arms his merchants better so that they cannot be taken so easily, or he lets them travel under the protection of warships. While in this way, the number of privateers increases, the ships which can be taken decreases, and consequently, the prospect for profit. As is generally the case with every lottery, many journeys are made where the costs exceed the profits. Even if at least some individuals make a prize or two, the vast majority of the adventurers lose. So the equipment costs during a war are greater than the total value of the stolen wares—then a nation loses all the work of so many to men engaged in raids, who also squander what they have taken through debauchery, drinking, and vices. They forget the sober habits of their earlier lives, and are seldom still good for business after peace. Instead, only the number of robbers and thieves multiplies. Even the entrepreneurs who had been so lucky to acquire a sudden fortune squander it again in senseless luxury. For the most part, their habits still persist even if the means for them are exhausted, and they are finally driven to ruin. Fair punishment for the destruction which they so nefariously and callously have afforded on so many innocent and decent traders and their families, whose activity was directed to serving the common interests of humanity."

On December 10, 1784, Thulemeyer confirmed receipt of the new draft and declared that he was personally in full agreement. "The 23rd article," he said, "is dictated by the purest zeal for the good of humanity. Nothing could be fairer than your remarks about the noble disinterestedness of the United States of America. It is to be desired that these sublime sentiments should be adopted by all maritime powers without exception. The calamities of war would then be considerably mitigated and the hostilities, so frequently evoked through greed or dirty profiteering, become less often repeated."

The Prussian envoy wrote to the king on the same day and noted that a translation of the draft treaty which Adams had given him was attached. "The newly added articles are the thirteenth and 23rd. Through the former, one has tried to overcome all the difficulties that so often arise regarding the concept and the nature of contraband. A special paper speaks in detail about the content and purpose of the 23rd article – refer to the above-shared memorandum, page 113. The American envoys, who aspire to reduce the misfortune of war in this way, think that those European powers who hurry to accept it in the interest of humanity would acquire an infinitely glorious title to the gratuity of mankind."

The king sent the American treaty draft to Schulenburg for his assessment, who first of all turned to the foreign ministers for their advice. Hertzberg and Finckenstein responded on December 17, 1784, "The major changes that the United States of America proposed in the thirteenth and 23rd articles of this commerce-treatise agree completely with the principles that we have maintained at all times. Particularly, that the king must not be guided by the ruin of the independent ship owners, but instead by the great end goal of obtaining a true and lasting peace. Therefore, piracy should be completely abolished or at least restricted as much as possible. Furthermore, if two powers wage war, the third does not have to suffer from it nor be responsible to give up their otherwise normal commerce. Consequently, none of the parties waging war have a right to take the goods of such neutral subjects if they do not directly serve to acts of war. As little should be taken from enemy ships in a besieged port as from a friendly or neutral ship. The suggestion of the United States goes still further, particularly to completely abolish piracy and war against unarmed people, and also not to confiscate contraband goods, but instead buy them from the owners or only prevent them from being supplied to the enemy. We believe that His Majesty can safely accept these suggestions since, in one part, it would honor your moderation, and in the other part, it is not foreseeable that you will ever be at war with the States of America or with another maritime power."

Schulenburg also spoke in similar words in his report to the king on December 24, 1784. This report is divided into three parts. The first required the resolution of some general concerns before the conclusion of the treaty can take place, while the second examined the separate provisions of the counter draft. The third subjected the new articles 13 and 23 to closer discussion and ultimately recommends their acceptance. At the beginning of his statement, the minister established the guiding principle that he does not touch further on any articles that correspond to the instructions given to him earlier and are in the Prussian draft. Instead, he only mentioned those which had been changed or newly added. He continued, "According to Your Majesty's instructions, the main goal of a trade agreement with the United States comprises of winning a secure and easy market for our linen, our woolen products, etc. and receiving Virginian tobacco, rice, and indigo as part of the value of these products in return. From this point of view, it was agreed that the ships and goods from the states of His Majesty should pay no higher levies in America than what vessels belonging to the most favored nations pay, and that if the Americans should give any preferential treatment to any other nation in the future, the same must also be extended immediately to the subjects of Your Majesty. The purpose of this latter provision is to maintain the balance of benefits, which could result in the granting of a reawakening national spirit to the English or the gratitude and friendship of the Americans to the French. It would enable us to always withstand the competition with English fabrics and woolen goods, as well as with Irish or Breton[60] linen."

"The American representatives' counter draft includes mostly all of the earlier articles, but it has given them a twist and added new clauses that remove almost all of the main advantages that Your Majesty expected from the treaty. In addition, it wants to establish freedom of trade that is too general to be brought into harmony with Your Majesty's states' applicable regulations and

60 Originating from Brittany, France.

practices. In this sense, articles 2, 3, 4, 5, 8, and 10 of the counter-draft require, in essence, that:

4. 1. The citizens of the United States of America can trade freely in goods of all sorts in all of Prussia.

5. 2. The products of Your Majesty's states shall only enjoy the benefits granted for them upon entry into America if they are imported in our own ships.

6. 3. The ships that have entered into a port or who see fit to leave such a port without unloading their cargo do not pay the slightest tax."

"I believe that, in compliance with the intentions of Your Majesty, a double constraint must be added to the first point. One, the Americans who want to trade with Prussia must subject themselves to the applicable laws and practices in the concerned destinations. The other, Your Majesty reserves the right, which is already stated in the fourth article, and which was completely omitted by the Americans in their counter draft, to ban the import or export of any items for reasons of state welfare. At the same time, the provision should be recommended to the satisfaction of the Americans that they should enjoy the same benefits if one or another nation is allowed the introduction of a product."

"Regarding the second point, Your Majesty has so often revealed to me that it is less your intention to expand the shipping of your subjects to distant ports than to secure a market for the national products. I might therefore assume that Your Majesty will never approve the clause held in the spirit of the English Navigation Act, according to which our goods should only enjoy the benefits granted to them if they are imported in our own ships. We must therefore absolutely insist that our goods are granted the same benefits no matter if they are imported in our own or in foreign ships. Regarding the third point, it seems fair to me that the American ships that enter our ports or sail out again without unloading their cargo should pay the same harbor dues or fees that other ships also pay for their better security and convenience.

According to my feeble insight, is it essential to insist on the restrictions outlined above and that if the Americans should not accept them, it would be better to not conclude at all than to sign an agreement, which in reality, procures no benefits to us. However, if the United States agrees with the above alterations, I dare to assure Your Majesty that the benefits are not merely mutual, but that your states will be victorious from this treaty."

He then critically examined the individual provisions of the counter draft and provided articles 2, 3, 4, 5, 8, 9, 10, 12, 19, 21, and 25 with his suggestions, which are given comprehensive consideration in the negotiations. In the statement following below, Schulenburg continued:

"The United States accepts the principle of armed neutrality in the most extensive sense, according to which the neutral ship determines the goods free, and even war munitions which are to be found on a neutral ship and are destined for the enemy are not confiscated, but instead can only be garrisoned. Your Majesty has already publicly acceded to armed neutrality, so this article will cause no difficulty. Apart from that, the treaty is dictated by that philosophical spirit that tried to reduce the calamities of war as much as possible. In the event that a war could break out between Your Majesty and the United States over the course of time, neither side will issue letters of marque for the disturbance of commerce. On the contrary, the merchant ship operators can even dock freely in an enemy harbor in wartime. Scholars, farmers, craftsmen, manufacturers, and sailors, etc., will not be bothered in the practice of their vocations: their property will be respected, and it will even sweeten the fate of the captives through inexpensive and humane measures. I confess that, given the position of the states of Your Majesty and that of the United States, most of these articles seem redundant to me. However, since the new American Republic ardently desires their acceptance by Your Majesty to establish the reputation of their humaneness and selflessness, perhaps Your Majesty will recognize, all the more easily now than in the event where these issues really should come into life, that his subjects would almost exclusively have the advantages of these articles. For it is easily feasible that the American privateers would cross into the North Sea, which already occurred in the last war, while there is not the least likelihood that Your Majesty would allow your subjects to send armed ships into American waters."

On December 29, 1784, the king thanked Schulenburg for his report and promised to make use of his remarks in the instructions for Thulemeyer, and sent these to the latter in the middle of January 1785. On January 24, the Prussian envoy informed the American representatives of the amendments and notes to their submitted draft from his government. For the most part, they only pertain to secondary points and mainly do not touch on those provisions that have rendered the Prussian-American treaty a name in the history of international law. While it is to the United States' credit that they inspired and first incorporated the treaty into a state document, it does not lessen the praise due to Frederick that he adopted it without any objection and even improved it with individual secondary provisions, which he did at a time when the Russian envoy in Paris did not once acknowledge the American initiations with a written reply, and Lord Dorset sneeringly rejected the propositions made to him by Congress because they were not at all legitimized to undertake agreements, and the power of the individual states must first be acquired. The negotiations are characterized by mutual courtesy and willingness to drop minor points. Overall, the American draft was elevated as the final treaty with only small additions and abridgments.

The negotiations took hardly three months, while the king dropped his objection that he held until the end against the nineteenth article on April 21, 1785. So, over the course of the summer, only a few individual formalities remained to be settled. The major points of the final adopted agreement along with the incorporated Prussian amendments are as follows:

After the first article expressed unbreakable, firm, and sincere friendship and peace between both powers, the second and third articles determined that the subjects or citizens of both contracting states may go to the coasts and territories of the other. They may live there and trade with all types of goods, products, and merchandise. The payment of customs and levies by them should not be higher than that of the most favored nations, and their rights and privileges are to be enjoyed in every matter. The king of Prussia put forward the addition that the traders are subjected to the respective country's laws and customs, which was approved by the United States.

The fourth article of the American draft stated that both parties shall have the right to bring their own products, wares, and goods in their own ships to any part of the other party's territory, where the subjects or citizens of the other could then buy them unhindered. Furthermore, they may freely purchase products, wares, and goods in the other party's territory for which they only had to pay the levies or duties paid by the most favored nations.

The Prussian side brought up three different objections against this article, these being: 1. That it gave permission to export all wares of a country without exception, 2. That it granted all persons the right to be a buyer or seller, 3. That it granted the right of transport only to the ships of both contracting sides and does not extend it to other ships.

To eliminate the first objection, the Americans later agreed to the addition that both parties can ban their subjects or citizens from the import or export of certain goods on the grounds of state welfare, and that if one of the two powers permits a third nation to import and export the banned goods, the other contracting nation's subjects or citizens shall enjoy the same freedom. Regarding the second objection, the commissioners noted that although the right to purchase and sell particular goods was the privilege of more preferred people according to one of the old practices in certain European countries, this practice's origins belong to a dark past. The general progress of time, however, required an improvement in this area. Trade has the important task of dispensing with surplus, satisfying shortage, and regulating prices according to a reasonable standard. It fulfills this mission best when it is at its most free. The wealthiest and most populated countries of Europe are those whose trade is the least restricted. Free competition between buyers and sellers seems to be the surest means to determine the true worth of a commodity. On the other hand, a monopoly is the most powerful means of stifling commerce. Therefore, both sides are interested to a high degree to steer clear of such a mistake in their agreement. The cited right enforced in Konigsberg that forbids a foreigner from selling his wares to someone other than native inhabitants is, to some extent, a monopoly. On the contrary, it seems to the Americans much more desirable that quite a few foreigners come to their ports and conduct their bartering there. His Prussian Majesty, who has already done so much to increase the good fortune of his subjects by removing more inhibiting barriers, may decide for himself if a reform of the Konigsberger statute is needed under the current circumstances. The principle of freedom of trade must be granted under all circumstances. However, they are willing to accept the addition that these articles should not restrict the particular laws of the city of Konigsberg that prohibit foreign trade within the city's territory. The king was persuaded of a better change by the Americans and yielded so much on this point that he even forbade the addition concerning Konigsberg.

Regarding the third objection, the Americans believed that a valuable improvement can be made in the free movement of goods if you secure the right of transport on your own ships. Both parties still maintain the right to deny this privilege to foreign ships, a right which was expected to only be exercised as retaliation against a narrow-minded nation. "We gladly abandon," it continued, "the reservation of our own ships since our aspiration is to completely emancipate trade and to provide all nations as much good fortune as possible through free trade. Hence, we agree to insert behind the words "in their own" (ships) the addition "or any other." Nevertheless, we would like you to consider if it is wise to completely abandon the right of retaliation towards a nation that restricts the cargo of ships to goods from their homeland. We, therefore, suggest an amendment to the topic: The contracting parties, however, reserve the right, if any nation restricts the transport of goods to the ships of the country that produced them, to exercise retaliation against such a nation."

The king also accepted this amendment and the addition "or

any other," so that, in the end, the article regulated the trade traffic between both nations in the interest of the greatest possible freedom of trade. It allowed them to import and export their products, wares, and goods with each other in their own or foreign ships without paying more than the levies and taxes charged to the most favored nations. At the same time, they reserved the right to exercise retaliation against a nation that restricts the transport of its wares to its own ships. Finally, it enacted the ban of imports and exports in the interest of state welfare. In this case, the citizens of the other contracting party would also not be allowed to procure the prohibited imports or exports. Prussia had suggested some modifications and abridgments to articles five through eight, which concern the port police regulations, to which the United States agreed. Likewise, they consented absolutely to the Prussian addition to article nine, which commands the inhabitants of one country to help and assist the stranded ships of the other, and stipulates the payment of such services that were carried out when the damaged cargo is unloaded. This addition, which consequently set up the closing of the article, reads: "The ancient and barbarous right to wrecks of the sea shall be entirely abolished with respect to the subjects or citizens of the two contracting parties" and had been justified by the Prussian ministers that, "this 'beach law' is still practiced against the stranded ships on most of the coasts of England in a barbaric style, regardless of whether it is forbidden by English laws, and that perhaps it can not yet be abolished entirely on the North American coasts either." Also, the American representatives set no opposition against the king of Prussia's desire that the prohibitions against the emigration of his subjects should remain unaffected and gave it a place at the end of the tenth article, which reflected the content of the eighth article in the Prussian draft.

This tenth article, which has also been included as Article XIV in the latest treaty, completed with Prussia from May 1, 1828, that is still in force today, claims a very special and practical interest under today's circumstances. It contains the more detailed provisions regarding the intestate and testamentary succession of the relatives of both countries. While it unconditionally recognizes the intestate and testamentary succession for movable property, it permits the undiminished sale of real estate only within a given deadline based on English common law, which also prevails in America, and makes foreigners unable to acquire immovable property under any legal title so that it falls to the state, and merely forbids the so-called detraction. At that time, this provision, which was doubly unjust because the Prussian law knew no such distinction, had little practical relevance. Today, however, when millions of Germans live in the United States, and the last-mentioned treaty even became law for the entire German federation on May 1, 1828; today, a German heir's pecuniary is hard-won by this medieval nonsense restriction whose elimination can not occur fast enough.

The eleventh article, which secured the absolute freedom of conscience and free religious practice, is an almost verbatim repetition of the seventh article of the first Prussian draft. The twelfth article was recognized as existing in force by both parties in the treaty of May 1, 1828. But only became a generally accepted principle of international law as §2 of the Paris Declaration of April 16, 1856. This article allowed free commerce of the neutral powers with the war belligerents and recognizes the tenet "free ship, free goods." The "free" ship protected all property and people contained on board, even the enemy, and only excluded the soldiers who stood in active service of the enemy. The end of this article, which recognized the tenet "unfree ship, unfree goods," was stricken out on the wish of the king of Prussia. This point stated that "Hostile ships shall also render the goods contained thereon as hostile so that what is found on board an enemy ship should be confiscated without distinction. Exempted are only such goods which are loaded before the declaration of war or within six months after."

This deletion was caused by the remarks of the Prussian ministers in their expert assessment presented to the king, "This stipulation stands neither in the same manner nor to the contrary of that in the royal Maritime-Neutrality-Convention, and as far as we know, nor in any of the Conventions concluded by other powers. We have always maintained, both in our public documents of the last and the previous naval war and especially in our circular declaration from August 30, 1781, that the non-contraband goods and goods not belonging to the necessities of war are not to be counted as hostile nor confiscatable, even on enemy ships, because a neutral nation would thereby be as little help to one war-waging side as it hurt the other in regards to the war. Even now we find ourselves in the position to reclaim non-forbidden wares for the Wroclaw merchant, Gottschalk, in Amsterdam, which a Dutch ship owner had taken from an English ship. So, we consider it necessary that the principle proposed by the American States at the end of article 12 not be accepted or acknowledged in our public commercial treaty and at least passed over and left undecided if we cannot obtain the expressed stipulation:

The effects and goods of one of the contracting parties which are found on board an enemy ship should only be subjected to removal and confiscation if they are determined to be contraband or are destined for the war, but that they be returned to the owner or can be purchased at a reasonable fixed price if they are the subject of a neutral power."

"We find this principle of the American States to be of the fairness and humaneness which they want to put as the foundation of the whole commerce treaty. It is so appropriate that we believe they would not reject it if it was properly presented to them and Sir von Thulemeyer was briefed about it."

Congress rejected this improvement. But it expanded the thirteenth article in accordance with the Prussian demand, which repealed the confiscation and condemnation of goods that were previously considered contraband and only allowed the stopping of ships loaded with them up to the point that if a ship is outraged in consequence of the delay caused by the so-called contraband, it may resume its journey peacefully and not be stopped any longer if it surrenders this contraband. Since this article and the 23rd are the most important of the whole treaty, it follows here in its literal transmission:

"And in the same case of one of the contracting parties being engaged in war with any other power, to prevent all the difficulties & misunderstandings that usually arise respecting the merchandise heretofore called contraband, such as arms, ammunition & military stores of every kind, no such articles carried in the vessels, or by the subjects or citizens of one of the parties to the enemies of the other, shall be deemed contraband, so as to induce confiscation or condemnation and a loss of property to individuals. Nevertheless, it shall be lawful to stop such vessels & articles, and to detain them for such length of time as the captors may think necessary to prevent the inconvenience or damage that might ensue from their proceeding, paying however a reasonable compensation for the loss such arrest shall occasion to the proprietors: And it shall further be allowed to use in the service of the captors, the whole or any part of the military stores so detained, paying the owners the full value of the same, to be ascertained by the current price at the place of its destination. But in the case supposed, of a vessel stopped for articles heretofore deemed contraband, if the master of the vessel stopped will deliver out the goods supposed to be of contraband nature, he shall be admitted to do it, and the vessel shall not in that case be carried into any port, nor further detained, but shall be allowed to proceed on her voyage."

Articles fourteen through eighteen concerned the harbor and maritime policing in times of war and peace. These provisions provoked no objections from either side. Thus, according to article fourteen, in the event of war, the ships of the neutral power should maintain sea letters or passes for the purpose of a more detailed indication of their nationality, their tonnage, and ownership. These are to be renewed as often as they return to port. Article fifteen stipulates the formalities under which warships or privateers of the war-waging power should approach and pay visit to the merchants of the neutral power. Article sixteen forbade the embargo or forcible restraint of the ships of one side in the event that the other considers it feasible in the interest of a military expedition of other public and private aims. Article seventeen ordered the return of the ships of the neutral power if they are taken by a warship of the other or a privateer of the enemy. They should be brought into the port of a contracting party. Article eighteen permitted the ships of one contracting party impelled by storms, pirates, or another coincidence to put into the port of the other power to re-equip and stock up on provisions under the pledge of more humane and kinder treatment.

The negotiations over the nineteenth article formed the subject of the most prolonged dispute among both parties. It granted them the mutual freedom to freely enter and exit a port of the other power with the prizes made in wartime by the armed ships or the privateers of one of the contracting powers without being forced to pay any tariffs, charges, or expenses to the concerned port officials. This point was also granted in the first Prussian draft (article 21) based on the Swedish agreement. However, in May of 1784, the Americans demanded that French prizes should be excluded from this provision because the older treaty completed with France compels the United States to make this concession. The king replied on May 24, 1784, in accordance with the views deployed in Schulenburg's memorandum, that it would be better if really no prizes at all were allowed entry into the ports of the contracting powers unless they were forced to do so by attack or bad weather.

Moreover, this permission was only beneficial to the Americans since Prussia neither has made nor will make prizes. The United States argued against the king's view that if one did not want to permit the entry into neutral ports with prizes, their position in a war with a European power would be very sorrowful because they must then return homewards over the ocean with every prize. Therefore, they restricted their stipulation so that only in the case of a storm or apparent danger can French prizes be brought into an American port. Frederick finally dropped his objection against this clause, which he considered completely impractical, on April 20, 1785, because the United States promised to not allow this exception created by the treaty of 1778 again after its expiration. Under this condition, he accepted the article in the form proposed. Article twenty forbade the contracting powers' subjects from receiving letters of marque from another state with which one of them is at war or providing assistance at sea or on land to them—failing which, they shall be considered as pirates. Article 21 stated the regulations to be observed in a war against a common enemy, particularly for the sale of prizes. In subsection four, the United States authorizes the condition set by Prussia that the courts of the place to which the prize is brought must determine their legality before sale. Article 22 specified that if the contracting powers have a common enemy or are both neutral, the warships of one which travels the same course as merchants of the other should accompany and protect them as if they were their own.

The 23rd article reproduced, partially verbatim, the recommendation of Franklin's above-mentioned memorandum. It read in its final version: "If war should arise between the two contracting parties, the merchants of either country residing in the other shall be allowed to remain nine months to collect their debts and settle their affairs, and may depart freely, carrying off all their effects without molestation or hindrance. And all women and children, scholars of every faculty, cultivators of the earth, artisans, manufacturers and fishermen unarmed and inhabiting unfortified towns, villages or places, and in general all others whose occupations are for the common subsistence and benefit of mankind, shall be allowed to continue their respective employments and shall not be molested in their persons, nor shall their houses or goods be burnt or otherwise destroyed, nor their fields wasted by the armed force of the enemy into whose power, by the events of war, they may happen to fall. But if anything is necessary to be taken from them for the use of such armed force, the same shall be paid for at a reasonable price. And all merchant and trading vessels employed in exchanging the products of different places and thereby rendering the necessities, conveniences and comforts of human life more easy to be obtained, shall be allowed to pass free and unmolested, and neither of the contracting powers shall grant or issue any commission to any private armed vessels empowering them to take or destroy such trading vessels or interrupt such commerce. The 24th article then proceeds: "And to prevent the destruction of prisoners of war by sending them into distant & inclement countries or by crowding them into close and noxious places, the two contracting parties solemnly pledge to each other and to the world that they will not adopt any such practice. That the prisoners of war whom they may take from the other, neither will send to the East Indies nor any other region of Asia or Africa, but that they shall be placed some part of their dominions in Europe or America in the respective territory of the contracting party in wholesome situations. That they shall not be confined in dungeons, prison ships, nor prisons, nor be put into irons, nor bound, nor otherwise restrained in the use of their limbs. That the officers shall be enlarged on their paroles within convenient districts and have comfortable quarters, and the common men be disposed in cantonments open and extensive enough for adequate fresh air exercise, and lodged in barracks as roomy and good as the soldiers of the power in whose control they find themselves. That the officers shall also be daily furnished by the party in whose power they are with as many rations and of the same articles and quality as are allowed by them, either in kind or by commutation, to officers of equal rank in their own army, and all others shall be daily furnished by them with such ration as they allow to a common soldier in their own service. The value whereof shall be paid by the other party on a mutual adjustment of accounts for the subsistence of prisoners at the close of the war and the said accounts shall not be mingled with, nor set off against any others, nor the balances due on them be withheld as a satisfaction or reprisal for any other article or for any other cause, real or pretended, whatever. That each party shall be allowed to keep a commissioner of prisoners of their own appointment with every separate cantonment of prisoners in possession of the other, who shall see the prisoners as often as he pleases, shall be allowed to receive and distribute whatever comforts may be sent to them by their friends and relatives, and shall be free to make his reports in open letters to those who employ him. But if any officer shall break his parole, or any other prisoner shall escape from the limits of his cantonment after they shall have been designated to him, such individual officer or other prisoner shall forfeit so much of the benefit of this article as provides for his enlargement on parole or cantonment. And it is herewith declared that neither the pretense that war dissolves all treaties, nor any other excuse shall be considered as annulling or suspending this and the next preceding article, but on the contrary that the state of war is precisely that for which they are provided, and during which that they are to be as sacredly observed as the most acknowledged articles in the law of nature or nations".

The 25th article authorized the employment of consuls, vice consuls, agents, and commissioners in the contracting powers' relevant ports. But upon Prussian suggestion subjects the mercantile consuls to the same laws and usages to which their nation's private individuals are subjected.

According to article 26, all benefits granted by one of the contracting powers to a third nation shall immediately become common to the other party. The 27th and last article finally set the treaty's duration to ten years from the day of ratification, with ratification occurring within one year from the day of its signing.

The contracting parties accommodated each other most kindly throughout the negotiations so that they could be finished in a relatively short time. This seriousness and zeal devoted towards the common cause caught the eye of the Americans as doubly beneficial against the tepidity and even callousness with which the other European powers either refused or set about to tackle the agreements offered to them. "I am," wrote John Adams to Thulemeyer on February 13 1785, "equally weary of the slow motions of the other courts and states as much as I admire the punctuality, intelligence, and determination of the Berlin court and as much as I am charmed to find that the king does us the honor to agree to the platonic philosophy of some of our articles which are at least a good lesson to mankind and will derive more influence from a treaty ratified by the king of Prussia than from the writings of Plato or Sir Thomas More. You can depend upon it that I will do everything in my power to bring this treaty to a speedy conclusion and, as far as my instructions allow, to conform everything with the observations of His Majesty."[61] Adams kept his word, and Thulemeyer also acted in the same accommodating manner.

As Thulemeyer announced the king's last concessions to the American representatives on May 3, 1785, he wished them and himself luck that the negotiations would advance quickly to a happy end. "The United States," he closed, "will certainly acknowledge the willingness with which the king has yielded in the different amendments of the trade agreement as new evidence that he wants to protect the trade and strengthen the ties which connect the Prussian subjects with the citizens of the republic. I anticipate for your and my country many lasting benefits from these new commercial relations which are built on the foundation

61 The Works of John Adams, Vol.VIII, 224.

of mutual responsibility and complete equality."

On May 26, 1785, in response to his letter, the American commissioners expressed to Mr von Thulemeyer their joy that all of the essential points were now finished, thanks to the king's goodness and flexibility. They only further requested that the treaty's duration be fixed at ten instead of fifteen years. The Prussian side agreed on July 8, 1785. The signing happened through the American proxies at their relevant places of residence. Franklin signed first on July 9, 1785, only two days before his departure from Paris to America. This execution was the last act of his diplomatic activities in Europe. Jefferson signed likewise in Paris on July 28, and Adams, in London, on August 5, where William Short of Virginia, the agent appointed specifically for this purpose, had brought the authentic copy. He then traveled to the Hague and presented the treaty fulfilled by the American party to the then United States charge d'affaires C. W. F. Dumas, who exchanged it there with Thulemeyer on September 10, 1785.

The king himself ratified the treaty two weeks later, on September 24, 1785. Adams and Jefferson sent the document to Congress for ratification. They said in a joint letter, dated from London on the 2nd and Paris on the 11th of October 1785, "We see with deep pleasure this union of our nation with a ruler, whose character gave a shine to every negotiation in which he took part. As this treaty may be of considerable importance to the United States and will certainly promote their reputation, it is to be wished that the ratifications may be exchanged, and the publication made as soon as possible. The admission of our privateers into the Prussian ports by a treaty signed at a moment when an alliance(German League of Princes) is being negotiated in which Brandenburg and Hanover (English) are parties,[62] is a little remarkable. It certainly merits the consideration of Congress and the states." John Jay, the then secretary of foreign affairs, submitted it to Congress on March 9, 1786, for ratification, who then also approved it.

How exaggerated were the expectations that both sides had for this treaty's effects and what vague ideas otherwise sober statesmen, matured through long standing experience, had about the driving forces in international dealings. This is demonstrated by the words of two men who reflect the dominant political views in their circles in the purest and most unadulterated light through their deeds and their spirit. Washington wrote on July 31, 1786, to Rochambeau and on August 15, 1786, to Lafayette: "Although I am not particularly well-versed concerning commercial affairs, nor have any foresight into scenes of the future, yet as a member of an infant empire, as philanthropist my character and, if I the term may be allowed the expression, as a citizen of the great republic of humanity at large, I cannot help turning my attention sometimes to this subject. I would be understood to mean that I cannot avoid reflecting with pleasure on the probable influence that commerce may hereafter have on human morals and society in general. On these occasions I consider how mankind might be connected like one great family in fraternal ties. I indulge a fond, perhaps an enthusiastic idea, that as the world is evidently much less barbarous than it has been, its development must still be progressive, that nations are becoming more humanized in their policy, that the objects of ambition and causes for hostility are daily diminishing. In short, the period is not very distant when the benefits of a

62 An alliance formed by Frederick the Great with other northern German rulers to oppose Joseph II of Austria's ambitions to possess Bavaria and cause a power shift in the German world, disrupting the status quo.

liberal and free commerce will, pretty generally, succeed the devastation & horrors of war. Some of the latest treaties that have been entered into and particularly that between the King of Prussia and the United States, seem to constitute a new era in negotiation and to promise the happy consequences I have just now been mentioning. It is perfectly original in many of its articles. It is the most liberal Treaty which has ever been entered into between independent powers, and should its principles be considered hereafter as the basis of connection between nations, it will contribute more fully to produce a general pacification than any measure hitherto attempted amongst mankind. Super added to this, we may safely assert that there is at present less war in the world than ever has been at any former period."[63]

Ewald Friedrich von Hertzberg, Prussia's great foreign minister, expressed himself to be completely in harmony with this in a letter to Washington dated Berlin, June 14, 1793: "I had the satisfaction, as cabinet minister, of approving the Treaty of Amity and Commerce concluded between the king of Prussia and the United States of America on September 10, 1785, in which you undoubtedly had a decisive part. I acknowledge that I have felt the greatest pleasure on seeing that your nation had looked upon King Frederick II as a worthy philosopher by making a proposition of this kind to him in order to give the example to other nations, and for the same reason I readily accepted it."

It might stand out that a ruler like Frederick knew better than any of his contemporaries that only the strongest battalions commanded respect and importance in the world and that hostile interests eventually can only be decided by the sword. It may be noticed that this king, who was always armed and ready on land, suddenly smoked the peace pipe at sea and wanted to

63 The Writings of George Washington, Vol.IX, 182 & 194.

replace the armed fist with the reasoning head there— murder and fire with philosophical postulate. However, it is very easy to explain his peace policy for obvious reasons. He knew very well that philosophical concepts could not replace naval power, which he possessed neither the means nor the will to establish. Only his fearsome position on land instilled respect from the naval powers and made him expect that they would not harass the Prussian merchants so easily in the event of a maritime war. Incidentally, Frederick had already proven in 1753 and energetically carried out how quickly he knew how to find the means to indemnify his subjects if the English prize courts unjustly condemned Prussian ships. In 1742, at the Treaty of Breslau, Prussia had taken over the repayment of a loan mortgaged on the duchies of Upper Silesia and Lower Silesia.[64] This loan had been transacted by Emperor Karl VI with London businessmen in 1735 to the sum of 1,700,000 Thalers. The most significant portion of this debt had already been paid off by Prussia towards the conclusion of the war at the end of 1748, when Prussian ships were being harassed by English warships and privateers in every conceivable manner. They were being dragged into English ports and condemned by the local admiralty courts or, if acquitted, were sentenced to pay the costs of the proceedings. The king protested in vain against these acts of force. He unsuccessfully evoked the English minister's frequent vow that the Prussian flag should be treated equally to the other allied powers. Frederick then decided to assess the loss inflicted on his shipping through a committee explicitly deployed for this purpose and to even wrangle justice. The damage was determined to be 194,725 Thalers, and the king deducted this amount from the

64 With the Treaty of Breslau, Prussia annexed most of Silesia and acquired these debts along with the land. Samuel von Cocceji was appointed to lead the legal restructuring of Silesia.

debt still owed to the English businessmen. This move naturally excited the most tremendous furor in all of Europe.

The king of Prussia, a ruler without any fleet, dared to pass judgment on the prizes of English privateers in Prussia! Frederick released a memorandum about this measure commanded by him. The English government wrote, as Montesquieu put it mockingly, a *réponse sans réplique.* The great Prussian jurist Cocceji appropriately responded to this. These legal statements, of course, convinced none of the arguing parties. Still, Frederick held the object of restitution of his subjects in his hands and could bide his time. This time came in the year 1756, as both powers concluded the neutrality agreement of Westminster. England agreed to pay 20,000 pounds sterling for the Prussian damages under the condition that the king removed the levy laid on the Silesian debt and paid the rest of it according to the original contract. This is what happened, and on June 23, 1756, the general acknowledgments could be exchanged.

But it should not be overlooked that the trend of the time, as the armed neutrality shows, pushed for the assertion of the rights of the smaller and medium maritime states against the monopoly of England. The king thus propped up his policies on a real existing political desire. His goals at sea appeared much easier to fulfill at that time than they later turned out to be. The federation against England had already disintegrated again before it had to endure the test of a great maritime war. But it had proved that, with more earnestness and more energy, an evenly-matched counterweight against England at sea could be created under certain circumstances, albeit a temporary unification of several interested parties. Also, the king could lose nothing even if his efforts remained a "beautiful abstraction." In the worst case, his policy was a seed for the future, a hint that could perhaps come to benefit his successors. In due time, this alliance with America was credited as one of the most humane acts of his long and blessed reign.

Considered by itself, uprooted from the connection with the political trends, an alliance of two powers who do not possess fleets exposes itself admittedly easy to the criticism of being a political Don Quixote,[65] whose motives were only justified and explained in the light of its time. The king had an army of 200,000 men behind him that would enforce his will at any moment and could be dangerous to the continental interests of the naval powers, especially England. Apart from that fact, the rulers and ruled, who were weary from all the previous fighting, still leaned almost abnormally towards peace just before the outbreak of the great European turbulence. They even considered everlasting peace to be possible. The king himself had already achieved so many significant results through diplomatic negotiations and mediations since the War of the Bavarian Succession. Why should he, who became increasingly more peaceful towards his end, not also expect universal recognition of international law principles, justified by peaceful means? Especially since the barbarism of the opposing determination was willingly recognized by the whole world.

It was in this peaceful idea of his political mission that Frederick coincided with Franklin. It's no mere coincidence that the philosopher of Sanssouci and the philosopher of the Poor Richard completed the last acts of their public service in Europe with the signing of the Treaty of Amity and Commerce.

But be that as it may, the treaty ratified by both sides expired

65 17th-century novel about a man who can't distinguish between fantasy and reality and begins to fashion himself as a real knight but usually ends up getting beaten back down to reality.

after ten years. Considering the minuscule and unimportant dealings that both states had with each other, neither of them gained any particular advantage from the treaty. They were also dealt with quite harshly by the war-waging naval powers in the next few years due to the treaty's general provisions concerning the rights of the neutral countries. When the conclusion of a new agreement was negotiated in 1796, the circumstances were significantly changed. The United States had risen from the inferior position that they occupied in 1785 to being state-regulated and able to develop their resources. While Prussia, living off its old glory, descended more with every day from its proud position of 1785, did not inspire any esteem from the world—neither through its force nor through its will.

On the other hand, the leading statesmen of the young Republic could not foresee such a fast upturn of the American trade at that time as it developed like a greenhouse due to the French Revolution. They overestimated the future via the prosperity of the present. They overlooked the fact that this was not due to normal development but that the European war had caused the blossoming of their trade. Meanwhile, John Adams became President of the United States and had just laid the foundation for an American war fleet. His son, John Quincy Adams, the later sixth President (1825-1829), was an envoy in Berlin at that time and was entrusted with the leadership of negotiations for the American side. The roles had become almost reversed. The president, John Adams, now expressed himself coldly and almost completely discouraged regarding the completion of an agreement. But in the face of approaching danger, he now dropped those exact points and improvements that had shaped Franklin's pride by their suggestion and enforcement. The instructions for

John Quincy Adams corresponded in accordance with this view of things.

"I am," wrote President Adams on September 14 1798 to his state secretary, T. Pickering, "not completely mortified about the delay of the treaties with Prussia or Sweden, having no ardent desire for any treaties until the crisis in Europe is more decided. It may not however be amiss to observe," he continued on September 30, "to Mr Adams (in Berlin), that he need not be solicitous about his success in making treaties with Prussia and Sweden at present. I am so fully convinced as he is, that both will affect to refuse any treaty upon the terms in his instructions. This will not alarm me at all, and if both powers finally refuse to agree to any stipulations without the articles in contemplation, we shall not be very unhappy. Our commerce is of more importance to them, than theirs to us, and with or without treaties we shall have all we want. But we should be very careful at the moment of being forced into a war to bind ourselves to permit France and her colonies to be supplied with everything, even our own produce, in Prussian and Swedish or Danish ships."

"The 23rd article of our old agreement"- closed Adams on May 13 1799 his discussion on this subject, "must be omitted from the new agreement. We can not waive the issuance of letters of marque. The legality of the privateers will not be set in question, however must one apply every precaution against the possible abuse driven thereby. The policy of privateering finds particular use to the United States. Our fleet is negligible and it will remain so for the foreseeable future, on the other hand are we strong through the number of our seafarers, through private wealth and through the unusual entrepreneurship of our citizens. Thus, the principal means of annoying a maritime nation would be our privateers. So, our strongest motive and fullest justification for using it would be that our extensive commerce, spreading and branching all over the seas, is more exposed than that of any other nation to depredations, both from pirates and maritime powers."[66]

According to these authoritative instructions from the president, John Quincy Adams left out some of the essential articles from the old treaty. "Experience having proved," so read article 12 of the new treaty from July 11 1799, ", that the principle adopted in the twelfth article of the treaty of 1785, according to which free ships make free goods, has not been sufficiently respected during the two last wars and especially in that which still continues, the two contracting parties propose, after the return of a general peace, to agree to concert with the great maritime Powers of Europe such arrangements and such permanent principles as may serve to consolidate the liberty and the safety of the neutral navigation and commerce in future wars. And if in the interval either of the contracting parties should be engaged in a war to which the other should remain neutral, the ships of war and privateers of the belligerent power shall conduct themselves towards the merchant vessels of the neutral power as favorably as the course of the war then existing may permit, observing the principles and rules of the law of nations generally acknowledged." Furthermore, contraband was defined in more detail and limited to weapons and war needs. Plus, the stipulation of the sixteenth article of the old treaty, which prohibited embargo, was repealed. Likewise, the original provision of the 23rd article was dropped, as far as it concerned the merchants and the issuance of letters of marque.

The third agreement, the Treaty of Commerce and Navigation, which is still valid today for all of northern Germany, was concluded by Prussia and the United States on May 1, 1828. It had

66 The Works of John Adams, Vol.VIII, 595, 598, 599, & 647.

decided the rights of neutral trade unfairly in favor of the Union. Its twelfth article specified that article 12 of the 1785 Treaty of Amity and Commerce and articles 13-24 of the Berlin treaty of 1799 were renewed with the same force and validity as if they formed a part of the present agreement. According to the old treaty, article 12 authorizes each of the contracting sides to trade with a nation that is waging war against the other contracting side and also recognizes the principle "Free ship, free goods." To avoid all of the usual difficulties and misunderstandings that emerge over contraband, article 13 of the treaty of 1799 further stated that in the event of war, all items such as weapons, munitions, and war supplies of every kind that are brought in on the ships or by the subjects or citizens of one power to the enemies of the other should not be counted as contraband. Therefore, they are neither confiscated nor condemned, nor cause loss to the concerned individual. The war belligerent can stop ships loaded with contraband and retain the goods that appear useful to them in exchange for payment for them, but must compensate the ship for losses suffered when it is released after the investigation has taken place. The end of the mentioned articles from May 1, 1828, finally said: "The parties being still desirous, in conformity with their intention declared in the twelfth article of the said treaty of 1799, to establish between themselves or in concert with other maritime Powers further provisions to ensure just protection and freedom to neutral navigation and commerce, and which may, at the same time, advance the cause of civilization and humanity, commit to again tread on this subject at some future and convenient period."

These good intentions have remained ever since. When Prussia completed this agreement, it did not have a single warship nor the intention of building a fleet, so its purpose exclusively benefited the Americans, whose possible clash with any European or other power always necessitated naval warfare to a higher or lesser degree. According to the existing international law doctrine (which was first set by England and likewise accepted as binding by the United States), a neutral government is not obligated to forbid its subjects from the sale of contraband to war belligerents although those that do so run the risk of becoming captured in transit. Thus, the Americans have the right to supply the enemies of Germany with weapons and war supplies, as stated in the treaty of May 1, 1828. However, Germany does not have the right to take private ships loaded with contraband from American citizens even if it possesses the means to do so. Instead, it must even compensate for their loss of time caused by delaying their travels if they do not want to buy the goods identified as contraband. According to the end of the 13th article of the treaty from July 11, 1799, items classed as contraband by both powers are canons, rifles, weapons of all types, and all war necessities. The war of 1870 has proven all too obviously for Germany what this stipulation means in practice. According to the wording of the treaties, the government of the United States absolutely did not trespass against their neutrality obligations when they sold about a million good rifles from their armories to the highest-bidding neutrals during this war. Which, of course, as we know, went to France and prolonged the futile resistance of the French by several weeks. If this pointless bloodshed was drawn out, the highly dubious credit could be attributed to the American republic. There is really no greater error than to celebrate the United States as the pioneer of the liberal aspirations in maritime law; they merely acted and behaved according to their current interests. They interpreted the international law as strictly as possible as soon as it served them as a war belligerent, while they gave the greatest possible expansion to the provisions that were in their favor as a neutral if they could make a profit from it. Their relation to the reform of maritime law can be examined more closely in the appendix. But here, as a final note, still a word about Prussia!

It had vigorously led the campaign of the "reasonable rights" against the maritime law, in theory, as well as in practice. The completed agreement between Frederick the Great and the United States was a promissory note for his successors, which they have sincerely paid. No law book of any nation had such humane and admirable regulations regarding the trade of neutrals and blockades as Prussian national law. Even if it could not abolish the privateering due to the lack of accommodation from the other powers, Prussia had already anticipated the other provisions of the Paris Declaration Respecting Maritime Law from April 16, 1856, at the end of the previous century. So decreed Part 1, Section 9, Portion 5 of the National Law, and particularly in the articles:

> §213. The property of the subjects of friendly or neutral powers found on enemy ships should not be detained (article 3 of the Paris Declaration).
>
> §214. Also, the property of enemy subjects, which is found on neutral ships is clear (article 2 of the mentioned Declaration).
>
> §219. A port is to be considered closed if it is blocked due to an enemy land battery or by warships that are stationed in front of the harbor (better than article 4 of the Paris Declaration).

The Prussian king's view regarding privateering can best be represented by a cabinet order from Wilhelm III, a prince not usually known for his liberal principles, that was issued on April 28, 1803.[67]

"I want to open with these words to you, that in a war, I am absolutely never willing to imitate the caper system of the naval powers that has extended beyond all limits in recent times. This is why the questionable addition seems to be completely unnecessary. In any case, it is not advisable to incorporate it into the common State Law. But it is necessary to reserve this provision for the case when the adamant need of the state might be forced to such measures that righteousness could otherwise never approve."

In 1854, on behalf of Friedrich Wilhelm IV, even Manteuffel declared for the abolition of privateering and sought to induce the United States to act in unison. In the wars of 1864, 1866, and 1870,[68] Prussia also renounced the capture and confiscation of enemy trade ships by its war vessels. It did so completely from the beginning of the latter war, but only under condition of reciprocity in the first two. Prussia and Germany are now often accused by the members of the naval powers that they only acted in self-interest, ideally to win an advantageous position for their unprotected trade or to secure the good opinion of the neutrals through compliance with this policy. This accusation does not apply because the greatest continental power of Europe, if they wanted to imitate their enemy's example, had very easily created a maritime militia without resorting to privateering that could take just as much from the opponent in their service even if not reliant on private booty, and even more harm would be done than by privateers or regular warships. Germany was poised to operate under these means when in 1867, war with France was threatened due to the Luxembourg Crisis. There was no shortage of suitable ships at

67 Ludwig von Rönne, Ergänzungen und Erläuterungen der preußischen Rechtsbücher, 5th Edition, Vol. I, 292.

68 Second Schleswig War, Austro-Prussian War, Franco-Prussian War.

that time, shortly after the termination of the American Civil War. The English blockade runners and other clippers out of service were much cheaper and more immediately available. There was certainly no shortage of experienced seafarers who would gladly and easily be recruited under the command of German naval officers. Germany had spurned this remedy in the last war and, albeit to the detriment of its mercantile navy, thus provided proof of the sincerity of its aspirations for the humanization of warfare at sea, which has not yet been sufficiently appreciated. When it finally abandoned its patience shortly before the end of the war, it did not sacrifice its previously asserted principles. In the long run, one can not dispense with the reciprocity in such wars. The single error that Germany had perhaps committed is that it had not made the reciprocity a condition of its renunciation of privateering from the start. Also, one should not overlook that the French navy and the fleet's heavy guns helped reinforce their land army, so it was essential for the German's success that they return them to their original professions. There was also the matter of subduing the French arms trade with the English and Americans. The eventual cancellation of the German declaration enacted at the start of the war was a measure that was primarily enacted for land warfare and would not have been done under any circumstances if it had been recognized in reciprocity by the French.[69]

But be that as it may, German authorities, chambers of commerce, and parliaments (the last in 1868) have fully provided the proof that they are serious with their efforts for the inviolability of

69 This passage refers to the Franco-Prussian War when Prussia had to resort to enlisting a private navy to counter the embargo by French ships on the North German coast, as the Federal Navy was not large enough to counter such a move. Having previously declared against privateering, Prussia was forced to renege on this declaration to deal with the French. Mr. Kapp explains and justifies this move.

private property at sea. For this reason, Germany is called upon, above all other powers, to seize the initiative for the reformation of maritime law during the imminent internal and external transformations of public law in Europe.

Supplement

The United States and Maritime Law

In the new international law literature, as well as in the manifestations of the German press and parliaments, it seemed to be good form to praise the United States as the intrepid pioneer of the advancements in maritime law—especially to exalt President Pierce and his Secretary of State, Marcy, as apostles of humanity due to them supposedly seizing the initiative on this issue. In being permitted to examine the stance of the United States in the maritime law issue unbiased against the facts, it is not with the intent to detract from actual merit or to fall back on men and matters in the past which have long ago been dismissed. On the contrary, it originates from the point of view that an austere assessment of Germany's policies towards America cannot be commended enough because the uncritical sentimentality regarding it seriously damages our national interests. Therefore, we begin with Pierce and Marcy, then conduct a short historical review of the country's foreign policy. We finally close our review with some highlights of its internal development.

Marcy has made a substantial reputation for himself in all of

Europe due to his critique and rejection of the Paris Declaration from April 16, 1856, which, as is well known, designated the last great tangible, formal, and universally accepted advancement in maritime law. Its short provisions read:

> §1. Privateering is and remains abolished.
>
> §2. The neutral flag covers enemy's goods, with the exception of contraband of war.
>
> §3. Neutral goods, with the exception of contraband of war, are not liable to capture under the enemy's flag.
>
> §4. Blockades, in order to be binding, must be effective, that is to say, maintained by a force sufficient really to prevent access to the coast of the enemy.

These clauses are by no means new but are found in individual state laws and, wholly or partially, in treaties and decisions of individual states since the days of armed neutrality (1780). Their real merit is that the minimum they offer is what the great naval powers could no longer withhold from the smaller naval powers' justified demands due to the sophisticated awareness of the time. While only applied sporadically or according to the mood of the stronger nations earlier on, these regulations now constituted an international law statute that could only be accepted by the states invited to join as a uniform, indivisible whole, but not in its separate clauses. Here we have the first beginnings of a codified international law, which is already a great victory in itself. But in the Paris Declaration, we also possess the reference point from which all endeavors directed to the further education of maritime law must originate when they have a practical goal in mind. Of course, since the days of their adoption, there have been many suggestions for the improvement and expansion of the individual clauses, and they have already grown into an impressive body of literature.

The history of the formation of the Paris Declaration can be summed up in a couple of sentences. Until the Crimean War, England had always been the most stubborn protagonist of the monopoly against the neutrals and had only reluctantly made small or temporary concessions in their moments of greatest need. England perceived a great danger in the Atlantic and Pacific oceans for its merchant navy. This needed to be averted at any cost due to the outbreak of this war and the obvious inclination of the United States towards Russia. As the happily shot arrow so often ricochets on its sender, they suddenly discovered that privateering, in the words of Clarendon to Buchanan, is a crime against modern civilization and temporarily renounced the issuance of caper letters. England united with France towards a common policy for even greater security, who themselves had often proceeded in the debatable maritime law issue, according to different principles. France thus renounced its supposed right to seize neutral goods under enemy flag. England, in return, on its likewise alleged right to seize enemy goods under neutral flag. How things stood regarding this latter so-called "right" of England is best illustrated in one of the English minister's, Sir William Molesworth, observations made in 1854. According to this, 119 out of the 130 treaties completed between the major powers of the civilized world in the previous two centuries had accepted this principle of "free ship, free goods." But only 11, among them 10 concluded by England, stipulated that enemy goods on board neutral ships could be seized. Even now, neither England nor France make it a principle, but rather only a temporary concession, and indeed for no other purpose than to avoid a great inconvenience and an even greater possible embarrassment. They achieved this goal because the United States and the European naval powers remained neutral in this short war and partially due to the issuance of caper letters being expressly renounced.

In 1856, at the Treaty of Paris, England and France found it in their interests to make the temporary concessions definite. They attempted to evade further and more urgent demands from the neutrals via installment payments that were virtually insignificant. If article one of the declaration did not prevent from committing piracy with their warships, the two following clauses neither renounced the right to search nor set any limits to the arbitrariness in the definition of the term "contraband." Finally, the regulations of article four were so loose and flexible about the effectiveness of a blockade that they left the door open to the hitherto exercised discretion of war belligerents and did not control the old abuses regarding the imposition and execution of a blockade in the least.

Out of all of the powers invited to the accession of this proclamation, only the United States raised a sensible and fundamental objection. They contested not so much against the three last clauses since they had always energetically advocated for concessions for the neutrals. However, they refused to acknowledge the first clause if the naval warfare, or in other words, state piracy, against private property was not given up. The allied powers rejected this condition because the declaration must be accepted in its entirety. They even gruffly rebuffed the Union government in 1862 when they sought to have the privateers of the rebels treated as pirates. But they still agreed to accept the complete undivided declaration.[70] Marcy's famous dispatch from July 28, 1856, elaborates on the standpoint of the United States in more detail. Even if it is essentially based on the principles already established earlier by John Quincy Adams and H. Clay, it is still a first-rate state document that will always claim an excellent place in the literature of international law.

In the first years of his ministry, Marcy was faced with the issue discussed here immediately after the outbreak of the Crimean War. At that time, Prussia had suggested to the United States that they expand the one-sided request from President Pierce to safeguard and regulate the rights of neutrals and simultaneously abolish the privateering. But Pierce explained in his annual address, edited by Marcy, from December 4, 1854, that he would only accept this proposal as an international statute if the removal of private property by the armed ships of war-waging powers was also renounced. The previously-mentioned Marcy dispatch followed this statement in the summer of 1856 and detailed the standpoint of the federal government at that time towards the Paris Declaration from April 16, 1856.

"The right to resort to privateers," it said, "is as clear as the right to use public armed ships, and as incontestable as any other right appertaining to belligerents. It is not denied that annoyances to neutral commerce, even abuses, have occasionally resulted from the practice of privateering, but when it is a question of changing a law the incidental evils are to be considered in connection with its benefits and advantages. If these benefits and advantages can be obtained in any other way without injury to other rights, these

70 Lincoln wanted Europe to recognize the rebel privateers as pirates but did not want to accept the declaration in its entirety for the Union. Thus, his request was rejected, but the United States would eventually agree to follow the Declaration of Paris (1856), years after the Civil War.

occasional abuses may then justify the change however firmly established may be the law. So far at least as operations on land are concerned, the persons and effects of non-combatants are to be respected. Every consideration which upholds this sentiment favors the application of the same rule to the persons and property of citizens found upon the ocean. It is fair to presume that the strong desire to ameliorate the severe usages of war by exempting private property at sea from hostile seizure to the same extent as it is exempted on land, was the chief inducement which led to the Congress of Paris declaration to abolish privateering. The United States joins in this endeavor gladly. They consider powerful navies and large standing armies as permanent establishments to be detrimental to national prosperity and dangerous to civil liberty. The policy of the United States has ever been adverse to such establishments, and they can never be brought to acquiesce in any change in international law which may render it necessary for them to maintain a powerful navy or large standing army in time of peace. It certainly should not excite the least surprise that strong naval powers be willing to forgo the practice, comparatively useless to them, of employing privateers upon condition that weaker powers agree to part with their most effective means of defending their maritime rights. How the United States must claim the aid of volunteers in their land warfare, so in naval warfare the privateers, the militias of the seas, replaces a strong fleet for them and protects their commerce. They are hence only in the case prepared to do away with the privateering if the European powers agree to the amendment that private property is exempted from seizure by public armed vessels. If such property is to remain exposed to seizure by ships belonging to the Navy of the adverse party, it is extremely difficult to perceive why it should not in like manner be exposed to seizure by privateers, which are in fact another branch of the public force of the nation commissioning them. According to the American view, no distinction between public piracy and private ships can be made. The piracy in general must stop, the state piracy along with the private privateering must be abolished. With adoption of the Paris Declaration would the power which has the strongest fleet monopolize the sea monopolize and permit interventions in the commerce of weaker nations which have a small fleet. No nation acts wisely that voluntarily surrenders the right to resort to any means sanctioned by international law which under any circumstances may be advantageously used for defense or aggression. If the United States renounced the right of privateers, it would be obliged to change its policy and assume a military attitude before the world, and thus would be attended with consequences most adverse to their commercial prosperity with any compensating advantages. The great naval powers however surrender nothing, but instead only gain if the smaller ones forgo the effective means to their defense. The ocean is the common property of all nations, and instead of yielding to a measure which will likely be to secure to a few an ascendancy over it, each should pertinaciously retain all the means it possesses to defend the common heritage. The United States can only accept the first article of the Paris Declaration if the amendment will be added that private property of a belligerent on the high seas shall be exempted from seizure by public armed vessels of the other belligerent, except that it be contraband."

This is the essential content of the Marcy dispatch. First, we envision the character of the man from which it originates and the government that its author so deftly represented. Marcy is most well known as Secretary of State and Foreign Minister under

Pierce (1853-1857). He was one of the most capable and most outstanding statesmen from one of the worst political schools, the so-called "Albany Regency,"[71] a creation of Martin van Buren. This corrupt clique had controlled the State of New York since the twenties and also exercised the most pernicious influence on the Union's political development. Principles in politics were worth just as little to them as the money a gambler risks at stake. There was no conscience for their members, no conviction of right and wrong. Instead, only political calculus. Their actions were merely the results of sharp mental acuity but directed on a narrow field, the unemotional calculation. Their goal was success, no matter at what cost it was won. The upper and lower politics were upper and lower hunts for these men, where they always did whatever could be done. Marcy was such an eager disciple of this school in his younger years that when Jackson took office in 1829, he deployed the sentence that has long been followed in practice as the principle that transferred privateering from the seas to the administrative offices of the state. The fateful doctrine that is practiced to a further extent with each day, therefore becoming more fatal for the United States: "To the victor belongs the spoils!" In German, this means, "The public offices are not filled according to knowledge, experience, and merit, but instead according to political practicality reasons. And only those that go along with the triumphant political party through thick and thin have a claim to an appointment, only to be thrown out again just as ruthlessly at the victory of the opponents." When Marcy joined the cabinet of Pierce, he had already been in very important and influential positions, such as the governor of his birth state,

71 Political machine that dominated New York state politics, which wielded power from influence, utilized the spoils system, and were known to profit financially from corruption.

New York, and war minister under Polk during the Mexican war.[72] He had proven himself as one of the most important heads of the country, as a man of extraordinary mental aptitude with especially sharp insight and sarcastic wit. In addition to this was an imposing exterior, a ruthless presence. A partially natural, partially adopted roughness with which he gained respect and obedience everywhere or used it to hold troublesome people at a more appropriate distance. In party politics, Marcy was always a conservative Democrat, later called an Old Hunker,[73] who had never been guilty of any heresy against the true Democratic church, i.e., the Southern tinted church. He was submissive to the beck and command of the Southern slave owner, the master of the political destinies. Yet, he always kept with his northern compatriots when possible. So, there he stood as one of the pillars of the orthodox democracy in the north and south.

A genuinely national man at a time when the democratic party threatened to crumble in the north. When Pierce became president, Marcy was especially agreeable to the victors orchestrated by the southerners because combined with his other good qualities was the illusion of independence, which he, in fact, did not have. Marcy also aspired to the Presidency and tried to reach it with the help of the southern votes. In doing so, this great talent could be all the better ensnared by the Southern politicians and be more thoroughly exploited for their purposes. Therefore, the slave owners gladly permitted his nomination but ensured that he stayed dependent on them by giving him three Northerners,

72 Mexican-American War.

73 Meaning "conservative Democrat," refers to the split within the Democratic party between the anti-slavery, small government "Barnburners" and the "Hunkers" who were pro-government and unconcerned with the slavery issue.

among them one decidedly southern-minded (Caleb Cushing); and three Southerners, among them Jefferson Davis, the later rebel President; as colleagues. Even if Marcy would kick against the pricks[74] here and there, he absolutely had to carry out the will of the Democratic party, i.e., the slave owners of the South. Only at subordinate opportunities did he have the choice to decide for the lesser of two evils.

The expansion of slavery both externally and internally constituted the central political focus and the exclusive topic of the Pierce administration. Internally, through the fighting which followed the enforced repeal of the Missouri Compromise by Douglas in his Nebraska-Kansas Act of 1854, they threw the last of the slavery self-consuming dynamite in bulk.[75] Externally, they tried to enlarge and strengthen the power of slavery through the acquisition of Cuba or transplant it to the middle of the continent through unauthorized interference in Central American commerce. Any other significant concern sank down as an irrelevant secondary point in relation to this all-dominant issue. But Marcy, who could do without privateering in a hypothetical hostile collision with Spain or with the great naval powers as little as he could do without freebooters[76] in the enforcement of his policy in Central America, would have raged against his own interest if he had renounced the private privateering. It would be war fleet

74 Resist; protest.

75 The Missouri Compromise had balanced slave and free states and limited the spread of slavery, but the Nebraska-Kansas Act created the territories of Nebraska and Kansas and allowed them to determine their slavery policy on their own, thus repealing the Missouri Compromise. Mr. Kapp alludes to the fact that this was the beginning of the end for slavery.

76 Also known as filibusters; irregular soldiers who executed unauthorized military expeditions to instigate and encourage revolutions or were used in government cover-up operations.

against war fleet in a naval war, and we need no further explanation for whoever might draw the short straw there.

A power advises in contradiction and acts against the requirements of its existence as soon as it enforces different principles and works with different factors in its external policies than in its internal policies. Marcy, who encouraged freebooters in the interest of slavery in his foreign policy in the Americas, would have become unfaithful to his own cause and suppressed the root of his strength if he had seriously campaigned the European powers for the freedom of the seas. In fact, nothing could be further from his mind, for he knew as well as any moralizing politician that piracy is the twin of slavery. Their mutual parents are robbery and theft committed against third parties, violence, and spoil, life, and enrichment attained not through work, but at the expense of others. The liberal mask that the Marcy representatives assumed in Europe cannot and must not blind us. They had a very flagrant interest in finding allies against the despotism of the Spanish queen because they wanted to have slavery with Cuba. They knew what they were doing when they declaimed against the intervention of third powers in the affairs of a country. They did not lie, but they only told the half-truth. They spoke of freedom, but they remained silent on slavery. They wanted freedom as the means, but slavery as the ultimate goal. How touching are these sly American politicians towards the devout naivety of the European revolutionary dilettantes, who imagined that they could exploit them for their own purposes! The burgher, Ledru-Rollin, exchanged letters with the citizen, Buchanan, who was then envoy of Marcy in London, and later was the worst and most contemptible president of the United States. He believed to be able to initiate a cordial agreement with the Republicans and slaveholders on the other side of the ocean. The *citoyens*[77] Pulzski and Kossuth dined with the *citoyens* Saunders and Sickles, two notorious New York politicians, the latter of which committed a wicked murder a couple years later,[78] and remarked about their meeting the same as one would an event of greater political scope. And so that the metropolitan bullfinches are not without the petty-bourgeois German, they teach uninformed travelers like the gentlemen, Mr. Wagner and Mr. Scherzer, their trusting readers, that "Poseidon Pierce shakes the mighty trident in the formidable fist and makes all tyrants of Europe quake on their thrones." In short, it was the idolatry of the phrase that the European republicans and penny-a-liners[79] pushed, while the agents of slavery pursued and achieved their very real aims.

This is not the place to accompany Pierce's foreign policies on their dirty wrong paths, to portray them with their threats and tricks, with their boastful approaches and cowardly withdrawals. The mere mentions of the Black Warrior Affair and the Ostend Manifesto, of the at-first refused and then later paid ships duties, of San Domingo's, the Sandwich Islands, the bombardments of Greytown, the freebooters Walker and Quitman.[80] These are all enough to characterize them. In short, this cabinet always swayed

77 French: 'citizen'. Used as a form of address during the revolutions in Europe of the time, signifying the desired abolition of titles and status. Mr. Kapp uses 'citizen' and 'burgher' in like fashion when referring to Buchanan and Ledru-Rollin.

78 Daniel Sickles was convicted of the shooting of Francis Scott Key's son, his wife's lover, in broad daylight across the street from the White House. Aside from being the first person in the U.S. to use the 'temporary insanity' plea, he was considered a hero for his chivalry and would continue to serve in Congress after receiving no jail time.

79 Hack writers.

80 Various episodes and blunders - mostly relating to Spain's possessions in Latin America and the Caribbean.

between greed and fear. And even if Marcy sometimes managed to quell the hot spurs under his colleagues and to bring the personally hated Jefferson Davis into the minority, he was still not strong enough to enforce an honest, trustworthy policy.

These internal reasons that called Marcy's good will in the reform of the maritime law into question are joined by external ones, which strikingly prove that he was not serious about the existing negotiations.

As the Crimean War broke out in the year 1853, it was naturally in the interest of the United States to not only defend their rights as neutrals, but also to expand them where possible. If American commerce had gained significant in-flowing cargo at earlier European wars and at the revolution of the Spanish-American colonies as a neutral, now even greater profits for the merchants and new markets for the producers stood in prospect. In the latter respect, they counted on the mass selling of American breadfruit and foodstuffs especially, which had grown into an important position in the world market since the last European war. The government originated all of their steps from this point of view, and nothing lay further from their minds initially, than to take a reforming position. In his message from December 4, 1854, Pierce gave the first official disclosure about his measures taken in this regard, which descended at the beginning of the year 1854. He said that the approval only temporarily declared by England and France of both clauses that were always recognized by the United States: "Free ship, free goods" and "enemy ships, free goods" was not enough. Which is why he had suggested to the other European and American governments to elevate these clauses as principles of the modern international law. Russia immediately agreed, as it had already concluded a treaty with the United States in July of 1854 in the spirit of this proposition. However, of the other great powers, Prussia had still requested the addition that they also mutually commit to the renunciation of privateering for the future alongside the acceptance of the plans. The President, due to the nature of the aid and defense means of the country, could not accept this proposition. The United States would only be willing to comply with them on this extended principle if the great European powers wanted to recognize that private property on the seas be protected from seizure by warships, just as by privateers, as a principle of international law. Pierce deployed the proposition; not to create a public opinion on this issue nor to win it for himself, but rather only to ward off an uncomfortable request. Had he and Marcy been serious with this statement, so had they forged the iron in the spring of 1854, when Clarendon (opposite Buchanan) declared privateering as a crime against humanity because England feared the American privateers, and did not shy away from sacrifice to win over the goodwill of the federal government for themselves. At that time, the threat and commencement of the equipping of privateers worked wonders and had significant practical consequences. Only the heads of the American politics had completely different tasks that were more important before them, as they were not satisfied with the temporary concessions made for the trade of the neutrals.

Approximately two years lay between that time and the Paris Peace. As Marcy writes his dispatch on July 28, 1856, Pierce was, despite his service performed to the southern barons, already eliminated with a foot kick and Buchanan, despised as a politician and hated as a rival by Marcy, was nominated by the Democratic party as the next presidential candidate. Of course, Marcy's days were now also numbered. He knew quite well that according to party practice he must make way for a successor to his foreign office seat on March 4, 1857. Fremont won the Republican nomination. But as was later the case, Buchanan won the Presidency. Thus, due to the personal enmity of both men against each other, Marcy was just as quickly eliminated, therefore, the utmost haste was necessary if he still wanted to achieve a diplomatic victory in the short period of seven months. But he was in no rush, because he had already attained what he had intended. This purpose had been to not be pressured into a detrimental, lopsided position by the European powers. In this respect his dispatch was a master stroke and a great diplomatic triumph which took the reins completely out of his opponent's hand. We hear Marcy's points of view in his own words: "If we had refused," he wrote on January 4 1857 to his envoy Dallas in London, "to accede to the Declaration of Paris on the sole ground that it abolished privateering, we should have fallen into a completely isolated position, as all other powers had given their approval to the whole Declaration. Our position before the world is now reversed; we shall, with perhaps the sole exception of England, have all nations with us. I would not, however, have made a proposal, to avoid the one or to ensure the other, which I did not think right in itself and generally in favour of the interests of our country." Incidentally, there was still a further step to make from this theoretical insight towards immediate practice. But Marcy felt reluctant to proceed diplomatically due to the turmoil in Central America maintained by Washington, which could lead to hostile action at any moment and require the issuance of caper letters.

On August 13, 1856, the dispatch from July 28 was communicated to the representatives of the United States abroad. The most important embassy post for this matter was London, which at that time was held by George M. Dallas as successor to Buchanan, who had returned to America on account of his presidency plans. Dallas was appointed in the spring of 1856, around the time when the Declaration of Paris was issued. He had always been known as an open opponent of Marcy on the issue of maritime law, and also had repeatedly expressed in his dispatches over the course of the year 1856 that, according to his view, the United States could not now or ever renounce the right of privateering. If Marcy was concerned with the success of the policies ascribed to him, he could not have acted more ineptly than to appoint Dallas as the representative of his views at that time. But Marcy was a very clever man, one of the most experienced politicians of his time. Therefore, we would do well, not to trust such naivety of him. He overrides any of our doubts in this regard via his instructions to Dallas, wherein he instructed to only bring the abolition of state privateering into the conversation with the English government, should he be prompted by its members. Now Dallas had to be a very incapable and inept diplomat, which he absolutely was not, if he didn't know how to avoid this subject in his negotiations with the English foreign office. He needed only to restrict himself to doing nothing, which he did, and Marcy contented himself to refute his envoy's views in private in the above-mentioned writing from January 4, 1857, more than five months after decree of the dispatch. Marcy likewise intentionally delayed and protracted the negotiations with France. That envoy Mason was there, who had written the notorious Ostend Manifesto (Acquisition of Cuba through purchase if possible, through force if necessary) and was later arrested with Slidell by Captain Charles Wilkes aboard the

RMS Trent as rebel emissaries.[81] Mason had decidedly good intentions regarding the present issue and the ambition to complete a treaty containing Marcy's request with the French government. On September 14, 1856, he submitted his proposals. Walewski repeatedly declared himself ready to conclude such an agreement in the event that England also wanted to. Mason now requested the appropriate steps from his colleagues in London but received the response from Dallas that he could not seize the initiative per his instructions. Marcy did not think it was worth the trouble to respond to the reports that Mason had made about his proceedings on this matter on September 17, and also on November 3, 7, and 17. He had only found time in February of 1857 to send his envoys in Paris the instructions and authority for the completion of a formal agreement with France, yet he did not even provide Dallas with the same order.

A couple of weeks later, on March 4, 1857, Buchanan took possession of the White House and Marcy, a worn-out man, made way for Cass and withdrew back into private life. The new government very soon completely dropped the maritime law reform after a few more suspicious rather than skillful twists. To have peace once and for all, Buchanan drew the bow still tighter and demanded, except for the Marcy proposal, the restriction of the blockade right in favor of the neutrals. A demand that, if seriously posed, would have of course, been absolutely refused by the maritime powers, with England at the fore. The perfidious intentions of the President were so blatant that even his envoys did not make the effort to cloak them. At the end of April 1857, Dallas even declared the statements made by Secretary of State Cass about the

81 Known as the 'Trent Affair,' a British vessel that was intercepted while carrying two Confederate diplomats to Europe where they hoped to solicit recognition and possible support.

expansion of the Marcy principles regarding blockade to the public as a mere mask to conceal the supposed change of opinion in his government. Buchanan, he remarked to the English ministers, came to the determined opinion that Marcy had gone too far with his proposals. That it was better to let the matter rest, since the United States could not give up the right of privateering as long as they did not possess strength equal to that of the English navy. For this reason, he was instructed to cease the negotiations concerning the maritime law issue.

Even the author of the meritorious writing, "Free Ships Under Enemy's Flag"[82] who otherwise always presupposed the honest intentions of the Washington government, began to open his eyes to this duplicity. "Under Pierce," he said, "the United States had tied the abolition of the privateer system to a condition concerning a further improvement. Now under Buchanan they tie the fulfillment of the condition set by them to another condition concerning yet another improvement. In the meantime, they kept always striding along to the peak of civilization and outpacing everything of humanity, but cannot dispense with the right of privateering that is abolished in the whole rest of the world because it is beneath their dignity to maintain a fleet for the protection of their coasts and their commerce."

The United States demonstrated how little they were, in fact, willing to renounce privateering a couple of years later through their policies during the Civil War. On March 3, 1863, Congress enacted a law valid for three years, the basis of which being the allowing of the president to issue letters of marque. Even if Lincoln made no use of this right, it still came about simply because the rebels had no ships on the seas, except for a few privateers.

82 "Free Ships Under Enemy's Flag" by Ludwig Karl Aegidi and Alfred Klauhold.

Incidentally, Sumner was the only senator who fundamentally objected to this bill, and during the discussion about it had suggested as substitute that the Minister of the Navy hire as many ships as necessary for the national service and, by placing them under the command of United States naval officers, should lend them unequivocal national brevet. "If the senators," said Sumner, "want to have a militia at sea, here it is. A sea militia, just like the land militia used in the service of the United States, who stand under their orders and receive provisions and payment from them. Instead of the pirates who stand neither in the service nor under the orders of the state and receive neither payment nor provisions from them. Pirates who, each in their own way, float around on the seas and without any higher commands, without any conformity of actions, are only ruled by the temptation for booty. Such a system would be immediately scrapped on land, nobody would call it a militia. Do not sanction it now on the ocean or, if you still want to despite all this, at least do not call it a maritime militia."

Sumner, of course, remained a preacher in the desert. But he was right because the authoritative goal of war belligerents must not be the booty taken from unarmed citizens, but rather the weakening inflicted on the forces of the enemy. The state which relies on privateering as its most effective and most indispensable means of altercation declares that it is too weak to protect its coasts and commerce through its own force. If the United States does not want to surrender their right to issuance of letters of marque against a weak enemy, how much lesser will they be against a possibly strong enemy? Their attitude even on this issue has - this cannot be emphasized enough - never been set in principle, but rather has always been determined by the present urgent concerns.

Among the statesmen of the revolution, it is mostly only

Franklin who tried to make propaganda for his "Quaker idea," as he called his endeavors for the humanization of maritime law. But he only penetrated Prussia with it. Congress allowed him to do so all the more, since due to its increased weakness to the point of helplessness, it could only gain through Franklin's policies. But as soon as real advantages were in prospect from a restriction of the same policies, Congress was immediately willing to limit his principal demands, if not to cancel them entirely. That John Adams himself behaved very coldly against the Franklin reform proposals is proven by his statements shared in the previous section. Jefferson put little weight on that issue, even though Franklin's aspirations in the area of maritime law corresponded to his French *Encyclopédiste*-leaning philosophical views. How little the majority of the American statesmen and politicians were touched by it is proven by the convention meeting in 1787 in Philadelphia, only two years after the treaty of 1785, which deliberated on the Constitution of the United States still valid today and included the authority of the issuance of letters of marque among the powers to be granted to Congress. As much as is evident from the main source for this period, "Elliot's Debates,"[83] there was not even one debate about this subject.[84]

When the French Revolutionary War with England broke out in the second presidential term of Washington, the United States naturally preferred to remain neutral and would gladly have enjoyed the benefits flowing from this position as long as possible. But now the war belligerents urged all the fiercer, each for themselves, for the participation of the Americans in the war. The United States' attempt to keep themselves out of firing range, yet

83 Two collections containing many documents regarding America's early days, compiled by historian Jonathan Elliot.

84 Elliot's Debates, Vol. V, 440, 510, & 511.

still encourage their commerce, entangled them into difficulties which became more threatening and troubling every day. It was folly to believe that in such an awful conflict of hostile interests, in such an embittered struggle of life and death, the egotistical commercial interests of such a young and weak nation were entitled to recognition. The United States was treated poorly enough by England and France because of this pretension. If they, like the European powers of the second tier, would not be drawn in with them into the abyss, they attributed it only to the conclusion that they were too insignificant and too weak, and that their alliance was in fact worth nothing. It would be going too far if we wanted to elaborate further on the intricacies of the policies that the Union spinelessly tossed around between the European belligerents from 1793-1812. Suffice it to say, that they actually had no policy at all, and took no position whatsoever on the maritime law issue, except for the weak attempts to assert their rights as neutrals.

Humiliations like those that the United States had to put up with from France and England during the last years of the previous century, had scarcely been taken by any Napoleonic Confederation of the Rhine.[85] And it served them right because their behavior was dishonest and false. They believed that the obligations imposed on them by the French alliance of 1778[86] could be revoked unpunished by leaning on England. However, they became enemies all the surer to both sides as a result. It is impossible to understand the American history of 1793-1812 if you do not take the Franco-American Alliance of 1778 and the

85 The Confederation of the Rhine was a confederation of German client states that were subordinate to the French Republic under Napoleon Bonaparte.

86 Referring to the Franco-American alliance made formal by the 1778 Treaty of Alliance.

policies of the United States that stood in contradiction of it as a starting point of the assessment. Washington's farewell address with its caution for "entangling alliances" indirectly draws its conclusion from the earlier errors committed. They could not grant the nation indemnity for the past, and only formed the creed of their foreign policy since the start of the nineteenth century.

Despite all impairments and chicanery by the war-waging powers, American commerce incidentally enjoyed an excessive blossoming at that time. Life was good for the merchants under neutrality because each year the continued hostilities increased the profit of the neutrals. The American navy never grew so fast as in the fourteen years from 1793 until 1807. At the start of this period at the outbreak of the French-English War in 1793, the contents of their merchant fleet amounted to 488,000 tons. As the United States threatened war with France in 1799, it had already grown to 939,483 tons. In 1807, shortly before the embargo imposed by Jefferson, it had increased to 1,208,735 tons. It then took a full 24 years before this height was reached again. In the year 1831, the gestation of the United States merchant navy purveyed 1,267,846 tons, though the population had doubled in this time.

In the meantime, the war between France and England became more and more bitter. The enemy powers mutually declared their countries to be in blockade status. The then-President Jefferson and his cabinet sympathized with France. They decided, in order to satisfy Napoleon, to exclude all American raw materials from England, thereby considerably damaged its commercial interests. The country-dominating Democratic party possessed their main strength in the agriculture-driven states of the south, whose later staple, cotton, still played no role in the world market at that time and had no idea about the laws and the development of commerce.

Their leader, Jefferson, had imparted the following wisdom about the trade policy of the United States in his notes about Virginia in the year 1785, "They ask me if it is advisable to support the efforts of our states, that it becomes a trading nation? If I could realize my own theory, so wished I that they engaged in neither trade nor shipping and were completely on the same footing as Europe, like China is doing."[87] Now as president, Jefferson realized this Chinese policy through the embargo which became the law of the land on December 22, 1807.[88] As a result of withdrawing all American ships from sea and holding them in the ports, it damaged the American interests most severely because it destroyed their own commerce and only encouraged the English, without winning over France. It is calculated that this errant policy of the United States cost 300 million dollars. A war would have been less expensive, and more importantly, would not have so deeply damaged the mental and political resilience of the nation. But this hiding from the theater of war did not satisfy the English. They now proceeded all the more ruthlessly against the Americans and their presumptions, and interventions went so far that the completely unprepared President Madison, for better or for worse, had to declare war in 1812. This second English war that now ensued was the price that the United States had to pay for their fluctuating stance, for their approach and their withdrawal, for their volition and incompetence in the maritime law issue. Only the Treaty of Ghent closed this sorrowful and humiliating period of their history for them.

It is imperative for our purpose to at least point to the main

87 A reference to the Canton System of China, which China used to control trade with the West within its territory and mitigate political and commercial threats from abroad.

88 Embargo Act of 1807.

events of 1793-1812. To provide proof through them, that the union was the unwilling pawn in the hands of the war belligerents a full thirty years after their treaty with Prussia. That they themselves didn't even know where their actual power and strength lay, and that they never acted according to clearly recognized principles, let alone dared to think of reform of the maritime law.

Only as a result of the rebellion of the Spanish colonies against Spain did the maritime law issue come to the foreground of public interest for the United States again. Monroe became president in the meantime, and John Quincy Adams stood at the forefront of foreign affairs as Secretary of State from 1817-1825, and from 1825-1829 as successor of Monroe as President. In the latter position, Henry Clay stood loyally beside him as Secretary of State. Adams, a more insightful and more experienced statesman, carried out a reasonable and excellent policy just as true and sensible as the interests of his country. While he behaved neutral in principle towards the European powers, he decidedly forbade their interference in American affairs and their colonization of American territories (Monroe-Doctrine) and intended a role as peaceful protector and leader for the United States towards the young, still underdeveloped, central and south American republics. In deliberate opposition to his predecessors, and in the full knowledge of the scope of his aspirations, Adams argued energetically for the abolition of private warfare at sea during the first nine years of his official activity, and took up the thread again where his father, President John Adams, had left off. The instructions issued by him to the American envoys; Rush in London from July 28, 1823, Sheldon in Paris from August 13, 1823, and Middleton in St. Petersburg from February 1, 1824 are classic examples of diplomatic notes and at the same time influenced by those ideal characteristics, which this excellent man so positively affected in all demonstrations. When Adams no longer lent his hitherto accustomed emphasis to his present endeavors in the summer of 1826 because they were received dismissively by England, Martin van Buren (Jackson's Secretary of State) again dropped the whole issue in his note from June 18, 1830, to Randolph, the envoy in St. Petersburg. "Since it would be a measure of very doubtful advisability if we wanted to limit the means of warfare at sea to our young fleet alone, the president thinks it more advisable to maintain, rather than to commit his country on an issue that is of such great significance to its safety." The then-envoy, James Buchanan, also wrote this message on May 30, 1832, to the Russian state chancellor, Count Nesselrode, that the American proposition for the abolition of private warfare at sea has been dropped since the

note directed to Middleton from February 1, 1824.

From Jackson until Pierce there was no more external instigation towards the Union, which could have forced them to take a stance on this issue. They remained, as always, with privateering as their most effective and legitimate defensive means. Summarized in a couple of sentences, the result of our examination emerges in the following:

The United States never had a firmly established policy on the subject of maritime law, let alone a reformed one. They appeared as if they were poor and helpless, like *dilettantes* of progress, who would drop this matter at the first prospect of profit in the interest of their commerce. After an almost thirty-year-old seesaw system, it was John Quincy Adams who first genuinely strove for the inviolability of private property at sea. Marcy eventually seemingly surpassed the European maritime powers in radicalism, but for all intents and purposes only made a clever maneuver with his motions for the abolition of the state privateering – to shift from the most unfavorable position possible to one as advantageous as possible.

Does this background offer any surety that the United States will energetically advocate for the suppression of privateering in the future? That they will connect with Germany in the direction of these aspired aims? One will do well not to indulge delusion in this regard because all signs speak for just the opposite of such a possibility.[89]

The United States, of course, is absolutely right if they act completely neutral with regards to European disputes and wars, and if they make their own national interests the sole measure of their policies. A natural and healthy national egotism is contingent on that it does not give up its defensive means as long as the possible enemy retains its own. Thus, in the present case it is a completely justified and clearly understandable requirement that the European powers must give up the state privateering at the same time if they desire the renunciation of privateering from the Union. So, the participation of the United States to the reform of maritime law can only be expected under the condition and prerequisite of reciprocity. Nevertheless, they might still refuse.

The United States stepped into a new arena of their development with the fortunate defeat of the rebellion. The fifty-year-old war against slavery and its subsequent elimination has to give way to some positives. Now the time has come to establish something new, no more simply destroying the outdated. For the Union, it matters above all to work their way up to becoming a great continental power and to become stronger from both the natural and gained conditions of its stately existence, not only towards Europe

89 From this point, Mr. Kapp begins to delve into the economical, political, and social circumstances of his day.

but also Asia. As such, they have common interests with the entire civilized world that require powerful action and can only seldom be reconciled with the neutrality recommended by Washington. With the jealousy of the colonies towards the motherland and the distrust against Europe which has formed the prevailing mood of the political relations of the United States with Europe even until now, it is no longer sufficient. No, they must take a stand on the cultural issues of the present and emphasize their views and interests. This mission found an ill-prepared generation before it. The leading politicians arrived at the helm simply through their position to the earlier, most important, issue of slavery. Whether or not they even had sense and understanding for political tasks is a completely menial question. Most of them possessed neither. Neither Johnson nor Grant, who have governed since the conclusion of the rebellion, have distinguished themselves through new inventive thoughts, nor by a clearer outlook than their predecessors. Their policies consisted of a persistent balancing and weighing of the various national interests and the local demands caused by them—of rumbling threats against England to coax the national prejudice and passions and minimize internal difficulties, and finally, of the witless repetitive old land haggling. The implementation of the Annexation of Santo Domingo[90] would have deflected the legitimate continental missions, required intervention in the West Indies tropical world and therefore, would have been a national disaster. In short, one becomes agitated at the unearthing of long since dismissed measures and goals.

Both of these presidents reflect exactly the average education and political opinions of the nation from which they emerged. If they did not rise up to the level of their assignment, the error

90 An attempt to annex the Dominican Republic by treaty, which failed due to low support.

lay less in them personally but rather in the limited views of their fellow Americans. They considered them merely as a means for local advancement of political or personal interests. They desire many privileges from them, but devote very few duties to them. This pernicious trend is expressed the strongest in the legislative power. In a country where merchants and lawyers decide the policies almost exclusively, it is primarily a mercantile, or a "shopkeeper" form of politics. Statesmanship has become a mere craft to them. This shopkeeper politics generates only party politicians who pass laws for one class, but creates no great statesmen who make laws for the nation and give their executive ideas which are turned into actions by the multitudes. Only politics that strive to realize the ethical and moral views or elevated passions of a nation in public and state life will be able to vaunt greater statesmen as the executors of their will. "A merely mercantile politician," said Theodore Parker, "can be very keen, indeed he can perhaps be very sharp-sighted, but his whole field of view is covered by a dollar and he can never again see through it." Any viewpoint reaching over the personal interests of the moment, any further laying issue, therefore the entire foreign politics, of course suffers under such a concept of state affairs. Nothing could be further from them than the approach to problems when the solution requires greater, more stately and more international goals. Politicians of that kind would therefore do nothing for the reform of maritime law, and we are forced to analyze the sources of their existence more closely, simply to provide evidence that the advancement of the inviolability of private property at sea can expect no support from them.

These men consider any political duty primarily as a deal to be completed as profitably as possible; a process which has to be won under any circumstances, and as a private speculation which could bring possible benefit. The means set in motion do not matter, only that they are successful. Loftier points of view are uncomfortable or even confusing to the view of the undecided and fluctuating, who have to be won over. "Is there money in it?" is the common question that the majority of the legislative proposals in Washington, as well as the seats of the state legislation face.

The representative only considers the common interests insofar as it does not stand in contradiction with his personal interests. In questionable cases, the former always give way to the latter. And being as it is not the entire country, without any provincial separation or limitation that forms the territory where the representative grew up, but rather only the narrower district of his native region, so his mental regard also shrinks from continental to parochial interests;[91] not the joyful approval of the people, but rather the endorsement of the provincial voters. Not the national welfare, but rather the satisfaction of the narrow wishes of the district. The considerations of self-gain form the standards of their workings. As cleverly as possible they avoid opposition and hostile claims, cling to powerful interests, and go along with the party through thick and thin. In brief, they must win votes and never lose. This purely personal mission consequently became the all-dominating purpose of their political bustle. The party machinery for votes, public rallies, etc. is in the hands of the most indifferent and often most corrupt local elements – political manipulators. They have but one obvious interest, to bring as many insignificant men as possible to the top so that they themselves can fish all the better in the murky water. Therefore, confident and significant

91 This provincial attitude permeated all walks of life and lasted well after the Civil War. Even Robert E. Lee, commander of the Confederate States Army, was against secession but wouldn't go against his home state of Virginia.

personalities are only sparsely disseminated in American politics, they are either silenced to death or isolated. The intelligence of the country, the intellectual life of the people is reliant on the activity in other arenas. Thus, whatever is noble and challenging in the United States is held far away in prudish, prideful seclusion from the political hustle and bustle.

In addition to these external reasons which bad lawmakers produced, there is the district system that is dominant in the entire Union, i.e. the custom practiced stricter than the law, according to which the elected delegate has to be a resident of the district voting for him. Accordingly, even the most important political head is dependent on the coincidence of the party colors of his place of residence. Which furthermore brings about the same habits and traditions that, with the same harshness as a bad law, only exceptionally sends representatives to Congress for longer than one term. The politics of the United States has a new face every couple of years, due to different ephemeral necessities and interests. Having said that, this change requires a greater degree of independence by the voters.

In no other country in the world are the legislation and executive branches as unadulterated by the expression of the feelings of the people or even the presiding national trend as in the United States. But the servility against the masses over the years has brought a democratic flood to foot which has shocked the foundation of the states themselves, the foundations of every orderly community. There is no longer any authority or any principle that spares the individual interests united by haggling, bargaining, and trading due to decency; the respective majority of which determines the internal and external politics of the nation.

New York and Brooklyn for example, which really only form

a single city with their 1.5 million inhabitants and has hundreds of outstanding men with proven character in all areas of knowledge, are normally represented in Congress by the scum of the big city population or the low politicians courted by the scum in their own personal interests. John Morrissey, infamous prize fighter and notorious owner of a gambling den, was representative of the richest commercial quarter of the city of New York for years.[92] With an annual budget that is greater than that of the kingdom of Bavaria, it is financially only a satrap of three of four Irish ward politicians of the worst kind, who hold all the threads and all political power in their hands, and the 40 city councilors who earlier were unceremoniously called "The Forty Thieves" and were lowered as mere registrars of the edicts of those ward politicians. In the year 1870, the ruling oligarchs even refused to make the annual account files and financial report public. To reassure the public, two millionaires had to declare that everything was in order after inspecting the accounts of the city treasurers, and therewith was the matter settled. In contrast, Tweed, the existing controller of the democratic flocks of New York,[93] distributed 50,000 dollars among the poor, and his colleague, O'Brien, gave them 5000 tons of coal, to keep themselves in power with the vote of the vermin. Of course, that was done with stolen monies, because about 15 million dollars were embezzled yearly from incoming taxes. "It seems in the realm of American politics that the law of modern industry prevails," said Hermann Raster, one of the most deserving and most spirited local journalists, "according to which the competition of the many is followed by the monopoly of the few. The machinery

92 Also known as "Old Smoke', Morrissey was a bare-knuckle boxer turned gambling den owner turned U.S congressman. He once even fought the famous gang leader, "Bill the Butcher."

93 William Tweed - boss of the Tammany Hall political machine.

becomes at the same time so immense and so complicated, that only a head connected with great capital can handle its management." Certainly, this example only affects New York, but the big inland cities hurry now to emulate the example of the authoritative metropolis even in this regard. So, this poison spreads from there out, welcomed everywhere, all the way to the most primitive municipality of the most distant West. The entire social and political bodies are affected by it. The infection may be faster here, slower there, but the whole country has absolutely fallen for this life-dominating idea of wanting to become rich without working. However, the backlash of this idea on the vast and foreign politics surrenders itself without any commentary. How can one expect to see the righteousness of the demand for the inviolability of private property at sea recognized by a nation that leads such an embittered war against the inviolability of public property on land?

This deterioration of the public spirit only came to light with the Missouri Compromise (1821), through which the slaveholders became the leading power in the states and began to rule over money and honor. It spread more every day to urban and parish affairs with the almost simultaneous expansion of general voting rights. It reached a higher level as a result of the unjust Mexican war, the discovery of California gold and the general commercial prosperity. But it rose even higher through the Civil War, which made colossal sums of money and profits in all channels of economic life, and generated the common view of all classes of society that the state only existed to exploit individuals for its own interests. The begrudgingly-worn shackles put on by important individual men and the undeveloped economic situation that daily grasps for more to exploit become weaker with every year. The last remains of the still strong bonds of family and community up until the introduction of "the steam"[94] was repressed by a democratized, purely outward equality. So now the stream of corruption unleashed everywhere is pouring devastation and destruction over the whole nation. In place of the southern land nobility, who the northern rabble took into its service, and in doing so commanded an alliance beneficial for both sides, steps the northern money nobility. These have at their disposal the means and ways a thousand-fold to draw the smallest backwoodsman into the vortex of doom without making him feel the immediate setback of the daily repeated attacks on the prosperity of the people.

Two years prior, one of the highest tax officials of the United States declared in front of the whole country, without encountering any contradiction at all, that it cost 100 million dollars to collect 300 million dollars net in direct taxes, due to the dishonesty and inability of the officials of the government. The mischief has become so strong that even the official politicians are so appalled by this system of looting that they strive for the example of European bureaucracy as the highest desirable aim for the civil service, particularly that of the German states. They also want to acquire honest and reliable service by proving knowledge and capability, with a public examination as the sole touchstone for the worthiness of the appointment. Tentatively, of course, these men aspiring to such a wholesome reform are found in the minority against the earlier-mentioned Marcy doctrine, that in politics "to the victor belong the spoils." They are powerless against the band of hungry office-hunters who are in no way inferior to the Clerici's of the late middle ages[95] in ignorance and insolence.

It would be laughable to believe that the United States could ever exist in the form of a monarchy. Apart from so many other

94 Steam locomotive.

95 Noble family from Milan.

reasons, the conflicting and opposing interests towards each other are already far too powerful to be capable of rising to the forefront of one person. The political future of the country will be determined by the already existing and new financial institutions, and transport companies emerging daily, such as banks, railroads and steamer lines. The financial and industrial activity of the present differs from earlier times in that the great capital must now be amassed in the hands of rich individuals or be accrued through association of lesser capitalists instead of being withdrawn from new activities, as it was in the past. It becomes more aggressive everywhere and it undertakes bolder conquests under the intelligent management of younger energetic forces. This changed character of capital doubly revolutionizes the old conditions in the United States because there are fewer external barriers here. Also, because it very frequently pushes men to the summit of big financial or transportation institutions who embody the audacity and daring of the nation less conscientiously than others and leave honor and shame behind them as superfluous baggage. Always pushing to the limits of criminal laws and often advancing past these limits without encountering isolation or the proper disdain in public opinion. To a nation of successful merchants, the actual concept of honor is completely lost. To them, the superficially immaculate gentleman is the ideal product of civic life.

Whoever in the Union has thoughtfully observed the vile activities of the railroad kings like Vanderbilt and Fisk, the Pacific Steamship Company, or the Camden and Amboy Railroad monopoly would not be able to escape the apprehension that the modern feudalism of the financial corporation, in its uninterrupted private war against the state, will paralyze and completely subjugate it in the end. The legislative and judicial powers have already become mere executors of the will of these mighty companies in many parts of the country. A cheeky railroad baron can openly and rightly boast that he owns a judge. Or a railroad company boasts with more cynical impudence and without falsehood that the legislature of a state belongs to them and that they can have a law created on demand in three hours, including the signature of the governor. To make matters worse, the government of the United States had given 186 million acres to the various railway companies in the year 1869 when they were about to approve the 1870 petition for a total of 190 million acres of federal land. If these companies still desire more with each day, one could easily get an idea of the overpowering position that substantiates these actions for the victor through means that are ever stronger on the side of the attacker and ever weaker on the side of the attacked.

But as the future may shape itself, this much is certain at the present. Beyond the purely personal and local points of view and their enforcement, the clearer, higher view of the common gets lost and the foreign politics of the United States suffer to the same degree, if not higher. Applied to the issue at hand, they will not so easily renounce the privateering, the state piracy.

For the time being, the hovering frictions with England must serve as the excuse if the proposal for reform is unceremoniously rejected. The charges against England are known to be founded on the damage inflicted on American commerce by English subjects through the assistance given in the equipping of rebel privateers. The raider, CSS Alabama, wreaked terrible devastation among the American ships from 1863-1864.[96] Since its construction and armament took place in forthright contradiction to the English neutrality laws, the Americans have, in this case, a legally

96 Commerce raider belonging to the Confederate States Navy that was built and equipped in England.

justified claim for compensation. Several comparable trials have remained unsuccessful because the United States government has posed their demands either too threatening or too far-reaching. The envoys Adams, Johnston, and Motley have still not gained any ground towards a peaceful settlement of the controversy. Henceforth, the newly-appointed envoy, Schenck, should reduce the expectations and declare that he would be satisfied with monetary compensation. It is possible, indeed probable, that this more peaceful policy will have better success and that a final settlement between both sides will take place. It happens, as is the evidence, that the statesmanlike view of victory has suffered, due to demagogic cravings in the Washington cabinet. Conversely, it is in the interest of the politician to keep this issue open as long as possible—because nothing in the United States is more popular, nothing more rewarding for every mindless, dull speaker and Congress politician than wild war cries against England. Everyone secretly or openly supports this power-driven political stupidity. Until now, the Union had the fortune of being directed by ministers who, like Seward during the rebellion war, reigned in the national passions in the decisive moment. But how long that will last is a different question. A war against England would be welcomed with true delight by the leading politicians. Or rather, the politicians adapted to the prevailing tone and by the criers of the tribunes and the pubs. The Irish, who number in the millions in the United States, are already so much merged with the Americans as a result of earlier mass immigration that one would do better to speak of Irish-Americans instead of Anglo-Americans. They are too valuable of allies to the party politicians that they will coax and accommodate them in every possible way. Favoring or even protecting the Irish prejudices, the blind suicidal indulgence for the daily more brazen than power-giving Catholicism, crude war cries against the natural enemy of the Irish – England. These are the indispensable sentences in the program of the politician who wants to have success. When a great meeting was held in New York for the celebration of the liberation of Italy from the political domination of the Pope,[97] only a single individual out of the Republican senators and representatives invited to participate dared to accept. The rest writhed like the devil in holy water. None of them wanted to affront the Irish.

If the leading men of the Republican party had possessed enough political insight to think beyond the needs of the moment, if they had even a shred of understanding for the members of foreign nations that settled in their territories, or if they had only made the effort to grasp their relative importance on grounds of the immigration statistics, they would have exerted everything to win the large German population of the country for themselves as a counterweight against the Irish, who vote with the Democrats. Numerically, they become more equal to the Irish by the day, if they are not already, and they will tower over them in the not-so-distant future because Germany is richer in emigrants than Ireland. But politicians have never seriously considered this goal, which lay in their own interests and those of the nation's future.

In political matters the Germans are more difficult to access and, due to their lack of knowledge of the English language, are also less helpful than the easily excitable and attainable Irish. At the same time, the Germans are useless because they are not so unscrupulous, not so reckless, and especially because they strive to become as financially independent as possible. However, the Germans are better citizens because they are more solid, more

97 Referring to the capture of Rome during the Risorgimento, which resulted in the debellation of the Papal States.

reliable and more prosperous, yet undemanding and more humble. Almost every German has at least enough of a conscience that he despises or at least distrusts those that make financial transactions out of politics. He has brought so much intellectual capital from the Fatherland with him that he at least dares to think for himself, and for the most part, does not follow behind every political bellwether like mere cattle, as the Irish do. So instead of gaining the Germans as allies, which would have been extremely easy from the days of the Nebraska Bill until the outbreak of the war, the Republican politicians only half-pulled them over to their side or repelled them completely through political blunders—like the partial support of the nativist aspirations and an amalgamation of state issues, such as temperance, Sunday-keeping and other such things. The leading German Republicans in every state of the Union have candidly striven to make the necessity of this alliance clear to their American friends, but they believe they can get by with installments and half measures, which start a couple weeks before the election and are discontinued the day after.

The Germans have become Republicans in their vast majority in the West, and enough is not said about the fact that they decided the first election of Lincoln to the presidency. Now the Republican party, which stands at the helm, throw themselves at the Irish to secure their domination, to whom they are just as antipathetic of their character as the bigoted Catholic is to the heretic. Even the President and Congress cottar[98] with them, because it is only about the "Ins & Outs"[99] to them. The highest federal official

98 Referring to the age-old practice of landowners leasing useless land to tenant farmers to be repaid in kind or labor. It seems Mr. Kapp is insinuating that the Republicans courted the Irish, but the only thing they were of any use for was votes.

99 Political, economic insiders vs. those on the outside.

of New York, himself an Irishman, drove like an emigrant runner in a United States steamship towards the Fenians, pardoned by England, in order to snatch them away right from under the nose of their business competitors, the enemy party.

The Germans are an extremely benevolent and vital counterweight against the American flexibility and carelessness in civic life due to their sedentariness, their style of small households, and that they form the most secure foundation of the state through the daily increase of medium and small property in their hands. Thus, they could also give American politics the character of greater stability and consistency, while the restless Irish-American element alienates the country more every day.

But the false policies of the government, which only envisaged ordinary election maneuvers, had a much greater range than its author was able to foresee. It is the worst blow that could be dealt to the nation. It is the careless abandonment of the pride built up from self-government in church and state which has given the country its substance and character from New England outward. As long as the aristocracy of the South has the interest to go hand-in-hand with the mob of the cities, this Irish alliance remains deeply in the progression of party politics. But if the party raised to the national government, which so gladly calls itself "the party of the moral conquests", seeks to supersede the Democrats and shack up with the Irish to keep themselves in office, so they commit a downright crime toward their people, because through this secession from the real root of the American power in their Protestant-Germanic base, and through their submission to Celtic-Roman influence, the natural development of the country would be interrupted, if not completely called into question.

The thoughtless, wasteful cries for war and revenge against

England, which are also rooted in the courting of the American parties towards the Irish, naturally do not allow the notions regarding the abandonment of private piracy to arise. The United States, so one reasons, could not give up the most effective means they have to combat England. But there is hardly any doubt that the Alabama Issue will soon be settled in one way or another.[100] Of course, then the external pretext of joining the agreement of the European powers for the abolition of piracy falls away. However, the Union will not be short of other, possibly more liberal, loopholes to whitewash their persistence in barbarity. From the American standpoint there are mainly two reasons asserted as to why it is for the best that everything remains the same. Privateering, for the United States, is at the same time the cheapest and mightiest, and therefore most national defensive means as a war belligerent, while as neutral, its retention brings immeasurable use and gain to them.

Concerning the first reason, the Americans are relatively mightier and more dangerous pirates than other nations by virtue of their natural dispositions—their daring, their lust for adventure, and their hunt for profits without equivalent work, as well as their technical skill in the building of lighter and faster ships. Therefore, the fact is that if they give up privateering, the advantage that they waive stands in bad proportion to the counter value that they receive. Like when they traveled in steamboats to Cape Horn at the discovery of the California gold,[101] when they sail on rafts or in the tiniest ships over the Atlantic Ocean due to a wager

100 This issue would be settled a year after the writing of this book, when in 1872, England agreed to pay the U.S $15.5 million.

101 Before the Panama Canal, a sea voyage to California necessitated sailing around South America's southernmost point. A common practice would be to venture through Central America's jungles to the Pacific and catch another ship to California.

or for sensations sake, so have they distinguished themselves from the first settlement of the Atlantic coasts onward as mariners and, when it is valid, as pirates. During the Revolutionary War, almost all sailors went on caper ships, and even craftsmen who led a sedentary lifestyle followed them. For example, in 1778 in Philadelphia no bookbinders were to be had because almost all of them were floating around on the seas as pirates. If a maritime war broke out, their privateers were equipped and ready for the hunt for booty quicker than the United States warships. The government need not first call on them, but rather could always count on them. Thus, they could skimp on their fleet. 'The more capers, all the fewer liners!' But even if the latter were much increased and improved, they still could not possibly take on the English fleet which was so superior to them. Now the United States could indeed take private ships into the civil service and man them with volunteers for the reinforcement of their navy, but they wanted to save on this expenditure and remain on a par with and dangerous to England at sea through their retention of private piracy. An estimated 100 million pounds sterling worth of English property was floating around on the seas at that time. In the year 1865, the value of exported British products alone amounted to 165,862,402 pounds sterling. What's more, England is always reliant on imports by sea for the nutrition of its dense population and for the procurement of the necessary raw materials for its factories (R. Schleiden, Reichstag Debate from April 18, 1868). Thus, the United States can do twice as much damage to England with its privateers than England can inflict upon them. But comparing war fleet against war fleet, England is twice as strong, if not still stronger, than the Union, and so the latter could lose just as much, if not more than they could win otherwise.

These views and calculations would perhaps yield better understanding and calm consideration from the statesman if the issue was deprived of the actual political agitation and, above all, of the commercial self-interest as a technical administrative measure. But this question of money and profit, the so-called "shipping interest," influences the Americans to speak out for the practice of privateering stronger and more imperative than the political question of power.

"It is our interest to remain neutral in a European war and to strive for the most possible extension of the rights of the neutral, but at the same time to reap the substantial advantages due to the neutral. It would simply be suicide to throw away the neutral advantages won after such a long fight by agreeing to the waiver of the capture of ship and cargo of war belligerents, because in such an event we would immediately forfeit our superiority as neutral over the merchant navy of the belligerents. If we approve a modification of the international law which also lets the trade of the belligerents continue in its old ways, we would lose the significant share of freight traffic that the European war brings to us. That may be a selfish consideration, but it is neither unjust nor does it stand in contradiction to the abstract law. The recently declared Prussian renunciation on capture and confiscation from enemy merchant ships is nothing other than a theater coup, an offer to the applause of a neutral audience." At the end is the old platitude used that through destruction of the enemy's trade, through as much damage as possible to the enemy's property, peace could be forced all the sooner.

These words are quoted from an article contained in No. 269 of the New York-based "The Nation" from the year 1870: "Freedom of Trade of Warring Parties". The Nation is the best-edited weekly publication, which has won it the most respected and most influential status among American newspapers through its witty polemics, sharp critique and rich content. That is why the above sentences have been cited from it, to which the approvals of less significant papers, the Chambers of Commerce, and political speakers could be added by the dozen. The reader may say to himself, what must the dry wood look like if such things already occurred when green. In the eyes of these critics, any attempt for a reduction of the hardships of war is the product of a feeble humanity, the solidarity of the international commercial interests but a fantasy, and pirates are possibly the apostles of civilization.

The European powers, one could further reason, can and will be drawn into a greater war all too easily. But the United States must be able to remain neutral in their favorable position and monopolize the freight trade of Europe as a result. However, this business would be lost if the war parties no longer needed to fear for their private property due to the abolition of privateering. Schleiden gave in his already-mentioned discourse some numbers which aptly illustrated these circumstances: "In the year 1865, arriving and departing the ports of the United Kingdom of Great Britain and Ireland: British ships for a gestation of 19,358,955 tons. 17,413,643 of these tons were filled with cargo. At the same time came in and out: foreign ships, for a gestation of 9,538,137 tons, and of that 7,572,202 tons were loaded. In the same moment when England is threatened with war, none of these British ships will dare to show themselves on the seas any longer. The Italian war has proven that insurance premiums increase at impending war, and nobody wants to charter English ships anymore. If we were to bring the posed principle (of the abolition of privateering) to recognition, the proportions in war times will remain pretty much the same as now. Ships of 19 million tons under English flag, and such of about 9.5 million under foreign flag will again come in, while in the event of war (at the retention of privateering) the proportions would certainly invert." Thus, the Americans would not have to be the good merchants that they really are if they were to give up privateering for such gains.

One does not argue against the fact that American Chambers of Commerce have already composed resolutions for the repeal of privateering. That is, however, a result of the Hanseatic suggestions and occurred under the action of excellent German merchants at the start of the year 1860 in New York, Baltimore and San Francisco. Mr. Leopold von Bierwirth in New York and Mr. A. Schumacher in Baltimore were the leading figures. Incidentally, the resolutions of these chambers of commerce did not prove much. They were at most the expression of the current prevailing trend and therefore won a certain moral influence.

At that time, individual American merchants believed themselves to be acting in accordance with the government when they stood up for the inviolability of private property at sea. But Buchanan taught them very quickly that their resolution could not be the subject of more serious consideration in the shape proposed. When the aforementioned Mr. von Bierwirth, in his patriotic enthusiasm for the welfare of the United States and Germany, again raised the same issue for consideration to the New York Chamber of Commerce in a masterfully-prepared submission on January 5, 1871, only a single vote besides himself declared in favor of the renunciation of privateering. All other votes were opposed. The biggest commercial newspaper in the United States, the New York Journal of Commerce, now even designates the proposal openly as an "Un-American Idea" and said, "Patriotism in itself is a beautiful thing and can do wonders, but when the greed for profit joins this standalone noble feeling as driving force, only then does it acquire double salary." Hence: long live piracy! But who does the Journal of Commerce reference with this gossip? How much national jealousy has to do with these views may be posed there. German establishments seize world trade for themselves and threaten to snatch up more and more. Even now, ten German ships arrive for one American ship in overseas trade.

Be that as it may, as much as the positive result of this investigation can be determined, the United States will withhold their consent to the abolition of privateering as long as their politics range in the current channels, both as war belligerent and as neutral.

Germany has now envisaged, as one of the provisions of the peace to be completed with France, the condition that both contracting parties not only renounce the capturing of private property at sea, but that they also should win over the other powers. Or, since the continental governments are agreed in principle, win over England and the United States for this doctrine. It is first and foremost a progress and a great relief that an agreement is being worked towards from state to state. This procedure is easier and above all, leads quicker to the goal. The examination to whether England will now comply to raise the freedom of private property at sea in wartime to a tenet of international law lay outside of the scope of the present task. It cannot be denied that an important change has occurred in England in relation to this issue during the last decade and it is very possible that even the attitude of the United States in the present moment can contribute to push England to the side of Germany. But this much seems certain, that it would be wasted effort to enter into negotiations with the United States before England has been won. If one still made this move, one would leave them two cards to play off of, and receive the most liberal assurances from them while they nevertheless persist in the maintaining of their old barbarism. The United States will only be forced to reveal their game when England joins the German point of view. If it does not do that, the negotiations with the Union are a fool's errand. But if Europe should reach an agreement on this issue, contrary to expectations, so may it also give the means, according to international law, to make accession extremely desirable to the United States.

Now the preceding analysis has hopefully proven that the popular beliefs and the supposed or true state interests discourage the Union from participation in the reform of maritime law. Indeed, they determine to prevent it. In the end, the question most often posed still remains to be answered. If, perhaps not out of humanitarian considerations but out of special friendship for Germany, they will join in the call for inviolability of private property at sea.

Even with this friendship, it has thus far not occurred. But in any case, it is very one-sided and only sought after by Germany. The United States earlier were and at the moment still are the great admirers and friends of Russia, with whom they very well will quarrel if their interests collide in the silent ocean someday. They dote on France, to whom above all the Irish-Americans gravitate towards. But that longstanding Irish population can't find any sympathy for Germany, even with the best intentions. That's why we would do better to not expect anything from a friendship that does not exist, because even if it does, it would generally levy no claim in the proceedings of the policies.

Unfortunately, the unhealthy draw, the sentimental reverberation of fatherland-less cosmopolitanism is still not extinguished in our nation and it compensates for the ailments of domestic affairs through overestimation and idealization of foreign countries and forms of government. The latest French experiment under Gambetta has stripped away the basis for this superficial view of European forms of government; at least for thinking men. The hollow revolutionary phrase has now finally fallen into deserved discredit, and the world begins to comprehend that not it is the figurehead, but the internal institutions of the establishment; not the cover, but the text of the book; in short not the external form, but the substance that must be the authoritative considerations for the appraisal of a state. However, the United States, at least for Germany, seems to still be the exception to this rule. One doesn't take the trouble to study their history and therefore endows them in naive ignorance with the halo of virtues and merits which, if really present, must be exalted to the appointed leaders for the stately advancement of their nations. It is already in private education a bad, long since dismissed method to retain model boys and make a fool of whipping boys. Nations hamper their own education in politics if they embrace this antiquated nonsense. The United States are the whipping boys for the conservative parties of Germany that are treated to an extra load. But to the great liberal majority, they are the model boys to be marveled at and envied. They are friendly-minded towards them, if not believing to be closely allied to them.

The German people and in part also the German governments have always devoted the warmest sympathies to the American Union. They have naturally taken this completely for granted, but they reciprocated it nowhere. The king of Prussia was the first European ruler who, at the outbreak of the latest Civil War, assured the government of Washington of his deepest commiseration. The German capitalists had such a firm confidence in the survival of the Union that they invested hundreds of millions in their promissory notes. The German masses welcomed the taking of Richmond as warmly as if it was their own victory. How have the United States answered? Not to mention the earlier events and the sympathy of the great majority of the Americans for the French, the federal government has, according to their own admission from President Grant, sold millions of weapons from their arsenals to the French agents during our present war where the French would be helpless without this support. They only stopped this disdainful haggling because the energetic protest of the German adoptive citizens made them fearful of a defeat in the next election. If the American government can escape the responsibility for their behavior, according to international law, through the silver engraved argument that they have sold the weapons to the citizens of their own country and not in any case directly to the French, German statesmen will now know what they are to make of this type of candid neutrality. Its cynical ruthlessness allows us and the whole world to now turn the complaints raised by the Union against England in the last few years against them in their entirety. The Washington government simply placed a commercial gain above the preservation of friendly relations with Germany, who they are not yet able to consider as the mightiest nation of Europe. As it is an Irish-American characteristic to bow down before the mighty and only to be harsh against the relatively weaker, so will also the correct realization come over time. In the present case, it is believed that one may still be harsh with impunity. Grant's prophecy made at the outbreak of the European war that this war would drive the price of American pork higher had not been realized, and also American grains were no more sought-after on the foreign markets. But something must be made from the war, and since the Germans didn't buy anything, they sold weapons to the French.

Therefore, no thinking man would be deceived about the purpose of the dispatch from February 7, 1871, through which the president recommends the Congress to convert the American legation in Berlin into a German one with higher pay.[102] Its purpose is simply so that Grant might cover his hasty withdrawal from the arms trading and suggest himself as friend and admirer of the German Empire. In the background might also have been the hope that the present envoy, who is no politician and the most competent since Wheaton, will be put out of office in favor of a politician through adoption of the proposed measure. The latter consideration does not concern us. For us, the weapons sales are the measure of the value of American friendship.

To the great majority of the American inborn inhabitants, the German is only "the damned Dutchman", because they think they are above them and do not go to the trouble to understand them. This national prejudice against Germany almost daily finds its approval in the actions of the government, and only seldom a rebuttal. The praiseworthy exceptions that the educated Americans make only confirm the rule. In light of these facts, the words of such an otherwise educated and witty historian, like Heinrich von Treitschke, sound like a downright mockery, when he said of the relationship of Germany to the Union, "The friendship which connects us with them arises not just from random diplomatic calculation, but from the feeling of a deep inner affinity that is awakened in both nations despite the difference of

---

102 Upgrading the office from a purely Prussian appointment to one for the whole of the German Empire, which was formed out of the various German states in 1871.

all ways of life in state and society."[103] If Mr. von Treitschke had said that Germany and the United States until now have missed all points of collision, he would have been right. But this relationship, purely negative and at times even hostile from the American side, can not be called friendship. A proper dose of mistrust towards the United States would be much more appropriate.

We Germans would do well after all, to not think too lightly of our relations to foreign countries—about the callousness and even partial contempt which we earlier had encountered too much, and fortunately have gotten out of through the hard work of the last seven years. But it is still due to the evil inheritance of our history, the small-state powerlessness and fragmentation, that we possess neither the trust nor the love of foreign nations. That does no harm. *Oderint dum metuant!*[104] A German policy based on justice towards ourselves and towards others, guided with self-confidence and power, even if not in the first attempt, will surely win us allies for the goals that we have posed to ourselves to achieve in national and general human interests. But let us count on the United States only as a last resort, if at all!

---

103 Preußische Jahrbücher, February Issue 1871, p. 187.

104 Latin: "Let them hate, so long as they fear!"

Appendix

Note:

I have taken the liberty to curate documents that were not in the original to better enlighten the reader. Contained in the original were both drafts of the 1785 treaty as well as the final version. As the drafts are covered in detail in a preceding section of the book, I have chosen to omit them and have instead opted to include various documents related to the subject matter. I hope they will be welcome additions and that the liberty I have taken here is justified.

—Joshua Lutz

A Treaty of Amity and Commerce, between His Majesty the King of Prussia and the United States of America.
Final Treaty from September 10, 1785.

His Majesty the King of Prussia, and the United States of America, desiring to fix, in a permanent and equitable manner, the rules to be observed in the intercourse and commerce they desire to establish between their respective countries; His Majesty and the United States have judged that the said end cannot be better obtained than by taking the most perfect equality and reciprocity for the basis of their agreement.

With this view, His Majesty the King of Prussia has nominated and constituted as his Plenipotentiary, the Baron Frederick William de Thulemeier, his Privy Counsellor of Embassy, and Envoy Extraordinary with their High Mightinesses the States General of the United Netherlands; and the United States have, on their part, given full powers to John Adams, Esquire, late one of their Ministers Plenipotentiary for negotiating a peace, heretofore a Delegate in Congress from the state of Massachusetts, and Chief Justice of the same, and now Minister Plenipotentiary of the United States with His Britannic Majesty; Doctor Benjamin Franklin, late Minister Plenipotentiary at the court of Versailles, and another of their Ministers Plenipotentiary for negotiating a peace; and Thomas Jefferson, heretofore a Delegate in Congress from the state of Virginia, and Governor of the said state, and now Minister Plenipotentiary of the United States at the court of His Most Christian Majesty, which respective Plenipotentiaries, after having exchanged their full powers, and on mature deliberation, have concluded, settle and signed the following articles.

ARTICLE I. There shall be a firm, inviolable and universal

peace and sincere friendship between His Majesty the King of Prussia, his heirs, successors and subjects, on the one part, and the United States of America, and their citizens, on the other, without exception of persons or places.

ARTICLE II. The subjects of his Majesty the King of Prussia may frequent all the coasts and countries of the United States of America, and reside and trade there in all sorts of produce, manufactures and merchandise; and shall pay within the said United States no other or greater duties, charges or fees whatsoever, than the most favoured nations are or shall be obliged to pay; and they shall enjoy all the rights, privileges and exemptions in navigation and commerce, which the most favoured nation does or shall enjoy; submitting themselves nevertheless to the laws and usages there established, and to which are submitted the citizens of the United States, and the citizens and subjects of the most favoured nations.

ARTICLE III. In like manner the citizens of the United States of America may frequent all the coasts and countries of his Majesty the King of Prussia, and reside and trade there in all sorts of produce, manufactures and merchandise, and shall pay in the dominions of his said Majesty no other or greater duties, charges or fees whatsoever than the most favoured nation is or shall be obliged to pay; and they shall enjoy all the rights, privileges and exemptions in navigation and commerce which the most favoured nation does or shall enjoy; submitting themselves nevertheless to the laws and usages there established, and to which are submitted the subjects of his Majesty the King of Prussia, and the subjects and citizens of the most favoured nations.

ARTICLE IV. More especially each party shall have a right to carry their own produce, manufactures and merchandise, in their own or any other vessels to any parts of the dominions of the other where it shall be lawful for all the subjects or citizens of that other freely to purchase them; and thence to take the produce, manufactures and merchandise of the other, which all the said citizens or subjects shall in like manner be free to sell them, paying in both cases such duties, charges and fees only, as are or shall be paid by the most favoured nation. Nevertheless the King of Prussia and the United States, and each of them, reserve to themselves the right, where any nation restrains the transportation of merchandise to the vessels of the country of which it is the growth or manufacture, to establish against such nations retaliating regulations; and also the right to prohibit, in their respective countries, the importation and exportation of all merchandise whatsoever, when reasons of state shall require it. In this case, the subjects or citizens of either of the contracting parties shall not import nor export the merchandise prohibited by the other; but if one of the contracting parties permits any other nation to import or export the same merchandise, the citizens or subjects of the other shall immediately enjoy the same liberty.

ARTICLE V. The merchants, commanders of vessels, or other subjects or citizens of either party, shall not, within the ports or jurisdiction of the other, be forced to unload any sort of merchandise into any other vessels, nor to receive them into their own nor to wait for their being loaded longer than they please.

ARTICLE VI. That the vessels of either party loading within the ports or jurisdiction of the other, mat not be uselessly harassed or detained, it is agreed, that all examinations of goods required by the laws, shall be made before they are laden on board the vessel, and that there shall be no examination after; nor shall the vessel be searched at any time, unless articles shall have been laden therein clandestinely and illegally, in which case the person by whose order they were carried on board, or who carried them without order, shall be liable to the laws of the land in which he is; but no other person shall be molested, nor shall any other goods, nor the vessel be seized or detained for that cause.

ARTICLE VII. Each party shall endeavour, by all the means in their power, to protect and defend all vessels and other effects belonging to the citizens or subjects of the other, which shall be within the extent of their jurisdiction, by sea or by land; and shall use all their efforts to recover, and cause to be restored to the right owners, their vessels and effects which shall be taken from them within the extent of their said jurisdiction.

ARTICLE VIII. The vessels of the subjects or citizens of either party, coming on any coast belonging to the other, but not willing to enter into port, or being entered into port, and not willing to unload their cargoes or break bulk, shall have liberty to depart and to pursue their voyage, without molestation, and without being obliged to render account of their cargo, or to pay any duties, charges or fees whatsoever, except those established for vessels entered into port, and appropriated to the maintenance of the port itself, or of other establishments for the safety and convenience of navigators, which duties, charges and fees shall be the same, and shall be paid on the same footing as in the case of subjects or citizens of the country where they are established.

ARTICLE IX. When any vessel of either party shall be wrecked, foundered or otherwise damaged on the coasts, or within the dominion of the other, their respective subjects or citizens shall receive, as well for themselves as for their vessels and effects, the same assistance which would be due to the inhabitants of the country where the damage happens, and shall pay the same charges and dues only as the said inhabitants would be subject to pay in a like case: and if the operations of repair shall require that the whole or any part of their cargo be unladed, they shall pay no duties, charges or fees on the part which they shall relade and carry away. The ancient and barbarous right to wrecks of the sea shall be entirely abolished, with respect to the subjects or citizens of the two contracting parties.

ARTICLE X. The citizens or subjects of each party shall have power to dispose of their personal goods within the jurisdiction of the other, by testament, donation or otherwise; and their representatives, being subjects or citizens of the other party, shall succeed to their said personal goods, whether by testament or ab intestato, and may take possession thereof either by themselves or by others acting for them, and dispose of the same at their will, paying such dues only as the inhabitants of the country wherein the said goods are, shall be subject to pay in like cases. And in case of the absence of the representative, such care shall be taken of the said goods, and for so long a time as would be taken of the goods of a native in like case, until the lawful owner may take measures for receiving them. And if question shall arise among several claimants to which of them the said goods belong, the same shall be decided finally by the laws and judges of the land wherein the said goods are. And where, on the death of any person holding real estate within the territories of the one party, such real estate would by the laws of the land descend on a citizen or subject of the other, were he not disqualified by alienage, such subject shall be allowed a reasonable time to sell the same, and to withdraw the proceeds without molestation, and exempt from all rights of detraction on the part of the government of the respective states. But this article shall not derogate in any manner from the force of the laws already published or hereafter to be published by his Majesty the King of Prussia, to prevent the emigration of his subjects.

ARTICLE XI. The most perfect freedom of conscience and of worship, is granted to the citizens or subjects of either party, within the jurisdiction of the other, without being liable to molestation in that respect, for any cause other than an insult on the religion of others. Moreover, when the subjects or citizens of the one party, shall die within the jurisdiction of the other, their bodies shall be buried in the usual burying grounds, or other decent and suitable places, and shall be protected from violation or disturbance.

ARTICLE XII. If one of the contracting parties should be engaged in war with any other power, the free intercourse and commerce of the subjects or citizens of the party remaining neuter with the belligerent powers, shall not be interrupted. On the contrary, in that case as in full peace, the vessels of the neutral party may navigate freely to and from the ports and on the coasts of the belligerent parties, free vessels making free goods, insomuch, that all things shall be adjudged free which shall be on board any vessel belonging to the neutral party, although such things belong to an enemy of the other; and the same freedom shall be extended to persons who shall be on board a free vessel, although they should be enemies to the other party, unless they be soldiers in actual service of such enemy.

ARTICLE XIII. And in the same case of one of the contracting parties being engaged in war with any other power, to prevent all the difficulties and misunderstandings that usually arise respecting the merchandise heretofore called contraband, such as arms, ammunition and military stores of every kind, no such articles carried in the vessels, or by the subjects or citizens of one of the parties to the enemies of the other, shall be deemed contraband, so as to induce confiscation or condemnation and a loss of property to individuals. Nevertheless, it shall be lawful to stop such vessels and articles, and to detain them for such length of time as the captors may thing necessary to prevent the inconvenience or damage that might ensue from their proceeding, paying however a reasonable compensation for the loss such arrest shall occasion to the proprietors: And it shall further be allowed to use in the service of the captors, the whole or any part of the military stores so detained, paying the owners the full value of the same, to be ascertained by the current price at the place of its destination. But in the case supposed, of a vessel stopped will deliver out the goods supposed to be of contraband nature, he shall be admitted to do it, and the vessel shall not in that case be carried into any port, nor further detained, but shall be allowed to proceed on her voyage.

ARTICLE XIV. And in the same case where one of the parties is engaged in war with another power, that the vessels of the neutral party may be readily and certainly known, it is agree, that they shall be provided with sealetters, or passports, which tenth of the said value where she shall have been longer, which sums shall be distributed in gratuities to the recaptors. 3. The restitution in the cases aforesaid, shall be after due proof of property, and surety given for the part to which the recaptors are entitled. 4. The vessels of war, public and private, of the two parties, shall be reciprocally admitted with their prizes into the respective ports of each; but the said prizes shall not be discharged nor sold there, until their legality shall have been decided, according to the laws and regulations of the states to which the captor belongs, but by the judicatures of the place into which the price shall have been conducted. 5. It shall be free to each party to make such regulations as they shall judge necessary for the conduct of their respective vessels of war, public and private, relative to the vessels which they shall take and carry into the ports of the two parties.

ARTICLE XXII. Where the parties shall have a common enemy, or shall both be neutral, the vessels of war of each shall, upon all occasions, take under their protection the vessels as long as they hold the same course, against all force and violence, in the same manner as they ought to protect and defend vessels belonging to the party of which they are.

ARTICLE XXIII. If war should arise between the two contracting parties, the merchants of either country, then residing in the other, shall be allowed to remain nine months to collect their debts and settle their affairs, and may depart freely, carrying off all their effects, without molestation or hindrance: And all women and children, scholars of every faculty, cultivators of the earth, artisans, manufacturers and fishermen unarmed and inhabiting unfortified towns, villages or places, and in general all others whose occupations are for the common subsistence and benefit of mankind, shall be allowed to continue their respective employments, and shall not be molested in their persons, nor shall their houses or goods be burnt, or otherwise destroyed, nor their fields wasted by the armed force of the enemy, into whose power, by the events of war, they may happen to fall; but if any thing is necessary to be taken from them for the use of such armed force, the same shall be paid for at a reasonable price. And all merchant and trading vessels employed in exchanging the products of different places, and thereby rendering the necessaries, conveniences and comforts of human life more easy to be obtained, and more general, shall be allowed to pass free and unmolested; and neither of the contracting powers shall grant or issue any commission to any private armed vessels, empowering them to take or destroy such trading vessels or interrupt such commerce.

ARTICLE XXIV. And to prevent the destruction of prisoners of war, by sending them into distant and inclement countries, or by crowding them into close and noxious places, the two contracting parties solemnly pledge themselves to each other, and to the world, that they will not adopt any such practice; that neither will send the prisoners whom they may take from the other into the East-Indies, or any other parts of Asia or Africa, but that they shall be placed in some part of their dominions in Europe or America, in wholesale situations; that they shall not be confined in dungeons, prison-ships, nor prisons, nor be put into irons, nor bound, nor otherwise restrained in the use of their limbs; that the officers shall be enlarged on their paroles within convenient districts, and have comfortable quarters, and the common men be disposed in cantonments open and extensive enough for air and exercise, and lodged in barracks as roomly and good as are provided by the party in whose power they are for their own troops; that the officers shall also be daily furnished by the party in whose power they are, with as many rations, and of the same articles and quality as are allowed by them, either in kind or by commutation, to officers of equal rank in their own army; and all others shall be daily furnished by them with such ration as they allow to a common soldier in their own service; the value whereof shall be paid by the other party on a mutual adjustment of accounts for the subsistence of prisoners at the close of the war; and the said accounts shall not be mingled with, or set off against any others, nor the balances due on them, be withheld as a satisfaction or reprisal for any other article, or for any other cause, real or pretended, whatever; that each party shall be allowed to keep a commissary of prisoners of their own appointment, with every separate cantonment of prisoners in possession of the other, which commissary shall see the prisoners as often as he pleases, shall be allowed to receive and distribute whatever comforts may be sent to them by their friends, and shall be free to make his reports in open letters to those who employ him; but if any officer shall break his parole, or any other prisoner shall escape from the limits of his cantonment, after they shall have been designated to him, such individual officer or other prisoner, shall forfeit so much of the benefit of this article as provides for his enlargement on parole or cantonment. And it is declared, that neither the pretence that war dissolves all treaties, nor any other whatever, shall be considered as annulling or suspending this and the next preceding article; but, on the contrary, that the state of war is precisely that for which they are provided, and during which they are to be as sacredly observed as the most acknowledged articles in the law of nature or nations.

ARTICLE XXV. The two contracting parties shall grant to each other the liberty of having each in the ports of the other, consuls, vice-consuls, agents and commissaries of their own appointment, whose functions shall be regulated by particular agreement whenever either party shall choose to make such appointment; but if any such consuls shall exercise commerce, they shall be submitted to the same laws and usages to which the private individuals of their nation are submitted in the same place.

ARTICLE XXVI. If either party shall hereafter grant to any other nation, any particular favour in navigation or commerce, it shall immediately become common to the other party, freely, where it is freely granted, to such other nation, or on yielding the compensation where such nation does the same.

ARTICLE XXVII. His Majesty the King of Prussia, and the United States of America, agree, that this treaty shall be in force during the term of ten years from the exchange of ratifications; and if the expiration of that term should happen during the course of a war between them, then the articles before provided for the regulation of their conduct during such a war, shall continue in force until the conclusion of the treaty which shall re-establish peace; and that this treaty shall be ratified on both sides, and the ratifications exchanged within one year from the day of its signature.

In testimony whereof, the Plenipotentiaries before mentioned, have hereto subscribed their names, and affixed their seals, at the places of their respective residence, and at the dates expressed under their several signatures.

A la Haye le 10 Septembre, 1785.	*F.G. de Thulemeier.*(L.S.)
London, August 5, 1785.	*John Adams.*(L.S.)
Passy, July 9, 1785.	*B. Franklin.*(L.S.)
Paris, July 28, 1785.	*Th. Jefferson.*(L.S.)

Declaration of Catherine II, Empress of Russia regarding the Principles of Armed Neutrality.[1] *Addressed to the courts of London, Versailles, and Madrid, February 28, 1780.*

The Empress of all the Russias so fully manifested her sentiments of justice, equity and moderation, and gave such evident proofs, during the course of the war she had to wage against the Ottoman Porte, of the regard she has for the rights of neutrality and the liberty of universal commerce, that all Europe can testify thereto. This conduct, as well as the principles of impartiality that she has displayed during the present war, justly inspired her with

1 "The Armed Neutralities of 1780 and 1800: A Collection of Official Documents Preceded by the Views of Representative Publicists" Edited by: James Brown Scott.

the fullest confidence that her subjects would peaceably enjoy the fruits of their industry and the advantages belonging to a neutral nation. Experience has nevertheless proved the contrary. Neither the above-mentioned considerations, nor regard for the universal law of nations, have prevented the subjects of Her Imperial Majesty from being often molested in their navigation, and stopped in their operations, by those of the belligerent Powers.

These hindrances to the liberty of trade in general, and to that of Russia in particular, are of a nature to excite the attention of all neutral nations. The Empress finds herself obliged therefore to free it by all the means compatible with her dignity and the well-being of her subjects; but, before she puts this into execution, and with a sincere intention to prevent any future infringements, she thought it but just to publish to all Europe the principles she means to follow, which are the most proper to prevent any misunderstanding, or any occurrences that may occasion it. Her Imperial Majesty does it with the more confidence, as she finds these principles imbedded in the primitive law of peoples on which every nation is entitled to rely, and which the belligerent Powers can not ignore without violating the laws of neutrality, and without disavowing the maxims they have adopted, notably, in different treaties and public engagements.

They are reducible to the following points:

1. That neutral vessels may navigate freely from port to port and along the coasts of the nations at war.

2. That the effects belonging to subjects of the said Powers at war shall be free on board neutral vessels, with the exception of contraband merchandise.

3. That, as to the specification of the above-mentioned

merchandise, the Empress holds to what is enumerated in the 10th and 11th articles of her treaty of commerce with Great Britain, extending her obligations to all the Powers at war.

4. That to determine what constitutes a blockaded port, this designation shall apply only to a port where the attacking Power has stationed its vessels sufficiently near and in such a way as to render access thereto clearly dangerous.

5. That these principles shall serve as a rule for proceedings and judgments as to the legality of prizes.

Her Imperial Majesty, in making these points public, does not hesitate to declare, that to maintain them, and to protect the honor of her flag, the security of the trade and navigation of her subjects, she is preparing a considerable part of her maritime forces. This measure will not, however, influence the strict neutrality she does observe, and will observe as long as she is not provoked and forced to pass the bounds of moderation and perfect impartiality. It is only in this extremity that her fleet will have orders to go wherever honor, interest, and need may require.

In giving this solemn assurance with the usual openness of her character, the Empress can not do other than promise herself that the belligerent Powers, convinced of the sentiments of justice and equity which animate her, will contribute towards the accomplishment of these salutary purposes, which manifestly tend to the good of all nations and to the advantage even of those at war; and that in consequence they will furnish their admiralties and commanding officers with instructions conformable to the above-mentioned principles, founded upon the primitive laws of people, and so often adopted in their conventions.

Resolution of the Continental Congress of the United States.[2]

Acceding to the Principles contained in the Declaration of the Empress of Russia, October 5, 1780.

Congress took into consideration the report of the committee on the motion relating to the propositions of the Empress of Russia; and thereupon came to the following resolutions:

Her Imperial Majesty of all the Russias, attentive to the freedom of commerce, and the rights of nations, in her declaration to the belligerent and neutral Powers, having proposed regulations, founded upon principles of justice, equity, and moderation, of which Their Most Christian and Catholic Majesties and most of the neutral maritime Powers of Europe, have declared their approbation;

Congress, willing to testify their regard to the rights of commerce, and their respect for the sovereign, who hath proposed and the the Powers that have approved the said regulations:

Resolved, That the Board of Admiralty prepare and report instructions for the commanders of armed vessels commissioned by the United States, conformable to the principles contained in the declaration of the Empress of all the Russias, on the rights of neutral vessels:

That the Ministers Plenipotentiary from the United States, if invited thereto, be and hereby are respectively empowered to accede to such regulations, conformable to the spirit of the said

2 "The Armed Neutralities of 1780 and 1800: A Collection of Official Documents Preceded by the Views of Representative Publicists" Edited by: James Brown Scott.

declaration, as may be agreed upon by the Congress expected to assemble in pursuance of the invitation of Her Imperial Majesty.

Ordered, That copies of the above resolutions be transmitted to the respective Ministers of the United States, at foreign Courts, and to the honorable the Minister Plenipotentiary of France.

British Instructions to the Commanders of Warships and Privateers.[3] *Containing the aforementioned Articles 10 & 11, November 20, 1780.*

An additional instruction to the commanders of all His Majesty's ships of war and privateers, that have, or may have, letters of marque against the French King, or the King of Spain, theirs vassals or subjects, or others inhabiting within any of their countries, territories, or dominions, or against any other enemies, or rebellious subjects of the Crown of Great Britain. Given at our Court at St. James's the twentieth day of November, 1780, in the twenty-first year of our reign.

Whereas, notwithstanding our former instructions to the several commanders aforesaid, some inconvenience has arisen from an ignorance of the nature and extent of our engagements with our good sister the Empress of all the Russias: we being determined to adhere strictly to the faith of those engagements, and solicitous to prevent, as much as possible, all illicit proceedings, do hereby enjoin to all the several commander aforesaid, the strictest observance of the stipulations of the 10th and 11th articles of the treaty of commerce, concluded between us and Her Imperial Majesty on the 20th of June, 1766, which articles are here inserted, that they

3 "The Armed Neutralities of 1780 and 1800: A Collection of Official Documents Preceded by the Views of Representative Publicists" Edited by: James Brown Scott.

may be accurately known to all the aforesaid commanders, and observed by them as an inviolable law.

ARTICLE 10

The subjects of the two high contracting Parties shall be at liberty to go, come, and trade freely with the States, with which one or other of the parties shall at this or at any future period be engaged in war, provided they do not carry warlike stores to the enemy.

This liberty, however, not to extend to places actually blocked up, or besieged, either by sea or land. At all other times, and with the single exception of warlike stores, the aforesaid subjects may transport to these places all sorts of merchandise, as well as passengers, without the least impediment. In the searching of merchant ships, men of war and privateers shall behave as favorably, as a state of actual war can possibly permit towards the most friendly neutral Powers, observing, as far as may be, the principles and maxims of the law of nations, that are generally acknowledged.

ARTICLE 11

All cannon, mortars, firearms, pistols, bombs, grenades, bullets, balls, fuses, flint, stones, matches, powder, saltpeter, sulphur, breastplates, pikes, swords, belts, cartouch-bags, saddles and bridles, beyond the quantity that may be necessary for the use of the ship, or beyond what every man serving on board the ship, and every passenger ought to have, shall be accounted ammunition or warlike stores, and if found shall be confiscated according to law, as contraband goods, or prohibited effects, but neither the ships nor passengers, nor the other merchandises found at the same time, shall be detained or hindered from prosecuting their voyage.

By His Majesty's command,

STORMONT

Convention between Russia and Prussia for the Maintenance of the Freedom of Neutral Commerce and Navigation.[4]

Prussia accedes to the system of Armed Neutrality, May 19, 1781.

This justice and equity of principles which Her Majesty the Empress of all the Russias adopted and acknowledged before Europe by her declaration from February 28, 1780, transmitted to all the belligerent Powers, have determined His Majesty the King of Prussia to take part as directly as possible in the glorious system of neutrality which has resulted therefrom, with the universal commendation of all the nations, not only by acknowledging these principles which are founded on justice and the law of nations, but also by acceding thereto and by guaranteeing them by a formal act. This determination of His Prussian Majesty meeting entirely with the desire of Her Imperial Majesty of all the Russias to give them a stable and solid basis by having them solemnly recognized by all the Powers as the only principles capable of establishing security of commerce and of navigation for neutral nations in general, Their Majesties have seen fit with one accord to enter into negotiations regarding a subject in which they are both equally interested, in so far as it can work to the welfare and advantage of their respective subjects, and to this end they have chosen, appointed, and authorized: His Majesty the King of Prussia, the Count von Goertz, his Minister of State, and his Minister Extraordinary at the Imperial Court of Russia; and her Imperial Majesty of all the Russias, Nikita Count Panin, her Privy Councilor, Senator, Chamberlain, and Chevalier of the

4 "The Armed Neutralities of 1780 and 1800: A Collection of Official Documents Preceded by the Views of Representative Publicists" Edited by: James Brown Scott.

Orders of St. Andrew, of St. Alexander-Newsky, and of St. Anne; Alexander de Besborodka, Major General of her Armies and Colonel commanding the Kiovia Regiment of Militia of Little Russia; and Pierre de Bacounin, her Councilor of State, Member of the department of Foreign Affairs, and Chevalier of the Order of St. Anne; who having exchanged their full powers, found to be in good and due form, have agreed upon the following articles:

ARTICLE 1

Their Majesties, being sincerely resolved to maintain relations of friendship and of the most perfect harmony with the Powers now at war and to continue the strictest and the most scrupulous neutrality, declare their desire to see to the most rigorous execution of the prohibition of commerce in contraband by their subjects, with any of the Powers now at war or which may hereafter enter into the war.

ARTICLE 2

To avoid any ambiguity and any misunderstanding regarding what is to be considered contraband, Her Majesty the Empress of all the Russias has declared that she recognizes as such only the goods included under this head in Articles 10 and 11 of her treaty of commerce with Great Britain, whose obligations, which are founded entirely on the natural law, she has extended to the Crowns of France and Spain, which countries have not heretofore bound themselves with her Empire by any engagement relating purely to commerce. Since there likewise exists no engagement of this nature between His Prussian Majesty and the Powers now at war, he declares for his part, that, in this respect, he also desires to bind himself with them by the obligations of the aforesaid treaty of commerce between Russia and Great Britain, with specific reference to Articles 10 and 11 of that treaty.

ARTICLE 3

Contraband determined and excluded from commerce, in conformity with Articles 10 and 11 of the aforesaid treaty concluded between Russia and Great Britain on June 20, 1766, His Majesty the King of Prussia and Her Imperial Majesty of all the Russias understand and desire that all other trade be and remain absolutely free on the basis of the general principles of the natural law, which Her Majesty the Empress has solemnly demanded, and of which freedom of commerce and of navigation, as well as the rights of neutral peoples, is a direct consequence; and in order that they may not depend upon an arbitrary interpretation, suggested by isolated and temporary interests, Her Imperial Majesty of all the Russias has adopted and established as a basis the four following points:

1. That all vessels may navigate freely from port to port and along the coasts of the nations at war.

2. That the effects belonging to subjects of the said Powers at war shall be free on board neutral vessels, with the exception of contraband merchandise.

3. That to determine what constitutes a blockaded port, this designation shall apply only to a port where the attacking Power has stationed its vessels sufficiently near and in such a way as to render access thereto clearly dangerous.

4. That neutral vessels may be detained only for just cause and when the facts are perfectly evident; that they shall be adjudged without delay; that the procedure shall always be uniform, prompt, and legal; and that, in addition to the compensation granted to vessels which have suffered loss without having been at fault, complete satisfaction shall in

each case be rendered for the insult to the flag.

His Majesty the King of Prussia accedes to these principles, adopts them also, and guarantees them in the most positive manner, binding himself to uphold them and demand their observance whenever the interests of the commerce and navigation of the subjects of the two high contracting Parties may so require.

ARTICLE 4

In return for this accession, Her Majesty the Empress of all the Russias will continue to protect the commerce and navigation of the Prussians with her fleets, as she has already agreed to do at the request of His Majesty the King of Prussia, having had orders sent to all the commanding officers of her squadrons to protect and defend against all insults and molestation the merchant ships of Prussia, which happen to be in their course, as being the vessels of a friendly and allied Power that strictly observes neutrality, it being understood, however, that the aforesaid vessels shall not be used for any illicit commerce, or for any purpose that is contrary to the rules of the strictest and most scrupulous neutrality.

ARTICLE 5

If it should happen, in spite of the greatest care on the part of the two contracting Powers for the observance by them of the most complete neutrality, that the merchant vessels of His Majesty the King of Prussia and of Her Imperial Majesty of all the Russias should be insulted, pillaged, or taken by the warships or private shipowners of any of the Powers at war, then the Minister of the injured party at the Court, whose warships or private shipowners shall have committed such acts, shall make representations, shall make claim for the captured merchant vessel, and shall insist upon suitable indemnities, never losing sight of reparation for the insult to the flag. The Minister of the other contracting Party shall join with him and support his complaint in the most energetic and efficacious manner, and they will thus act with one accord. If justice should be refused, or if it should be postponed from time to time, then Their Majesties shall employ reprisals against the Power so refusing and they shall continually consult with each other as to the most appropriate method for carrying out such reprisals.

ARTICLE 6

If it should happen that either of the two contracting Powers or both of them, because of or in contempt of the present act, or for any other cause relating thereto, should be disturbed, molested, or attacked, it has been likewise agreed that the two powers shall make common cause for their mutual defense, and shall work and act in concert in order to secure entire and full satisfaction, both for the insult to their flag and for the losses caused to their subjects.

ARTICLE 7

The present act shall have no retroactive effect, and therefore no action shall be taken with respect to differences that have arisen before its conclusion, unless it is a question of continuous acts of violence, tending to establish an oppressive system for all the neutral countries of Europe in general.

ARTICLE 8

All the stipulations set forth in the present act must be regarded as permanent and as constituting the law in the matter of commerce and of navigation, and whenever there is occasion to determine the rights of neutral nations.

ARTICLE 9

The principal aim and object of this act being to ensure general freedom of commerce and of navigation, His Prussian Majesty and Her Imperial Majesty of all the Russias agree and engage in advance to allow other neutral Powers to accede hereto, which by adopting the principles herein contained shall share its obligations as well as its advantages.

ARTICLE 10

In order that the Powers at war may not allege their ignorance of the engagements undertaken by Their said Majesties, they shall communicate in a friendly way to the said Powers these engagements, which are in nowise hostile to them nor to the detriment of any one of them, but aim solely to ensure security of commerce and of navigation to their respective subjects.

ARTICLE 11

The present act shall be ratified by the two contracting Parties, and the ratifications thereof shall be exchanged within six weeks from the day of the signing thereof, or sooner if possible.

In faith whereof we, the plenipotentiaries, by virtue of our full Powers have signed and have hereto affixed the seals of our arms.

Done at St. Petersburg, May 8, 1781.

(L.S.) E. Count von Goertz
(L.S.) C. N. Panin
(L.S.) C. John D'Ostermann
(L.S.) Alexander de Besborodka
(L.S.) Pierre de Bacounin

Separate Articles

ARTICLE 1

As His Majesty the King of Prussia and Her Majesty the Empress of all the Russias are equally interested in preserving the security and tranquility of the Baltic Sea, and in protecting it from the disturbances of war and privateering, a system the more just and natural because the Powers whose States border thereon enjoy the most profound peace. They have mutually agreed to maintain that it is a closed sea, incontestably such by its geographical situation, in which all nations must and may navigate in peace and enjoy all the advantages of perfect tranquillity, and to this end to adopt among themselves measures capable of guaranteeing this sea and its coasts against all hostilities, piracies, and acts of violence.

ARTICLE 2

Since stress of weather or some other circumstance may force Russian vessels to take refuge in a Prussian port, either to pass the winter, to make repairs, or to escape the storm, His Majesty the King of Prussia engages to see to it that they are furnished, at a just and reasonable price, with the necessary materials for repairs and with the provisions needed by the crew for its sustenance; in a word, to see that all necessary arrangements are made in order that these vessels and their crews may be treated and cared for in the most friendly manner.

ARTICLE 3

At the more or less remote time when peace shall be restored between the belligerent Powers, His Majesty the King of Prussia and Her Majesty the Empress of all the Russias shall use their best efforts with the maritime Powers in general to bring about the universal acceptance and recognition in all naval wars, which may arise hereafter, of the system of neutrality and the principles established in the present act, forming the basis of a universal maritime code.

ARTICLE 4

As soon as this act shall have been ratified and the exchange of ratifications shall have taken place, the high contracting Powers shall take care to communicate it, with the exception of the separate articles, in good faith, conjointly and with one accord, through their Ministers accredited to foreign Courts, and specifically those Courts which are now at war.

These separate articles shall be considered and regarded as forming a part of the act itself and shall have the same force and effect as though they had been inserted word for word in the said act, concluded the same day between the two high contracting Parties. They shall be ratified in the say way and ratifications thereof shall be exchanged at the same time.

In faith whereof we, the plenipotentiaries, by virtue of our full powers, have signed them and have affixed thereto the seals of our arms.

Done at St. Petersburg, May 8, 1781.

(L.S.) E. Count von Goertz
(L.S.) C. N. Panin
(L.S.) C. John D'Ostermann
(L.S.) Alexander de Besborodka
(L.S.) Pierre de Bacounin

Instructions to the Commanders of Private Ships or Vessels of War, which shall have Commissions or Letters of Marque and Reprisal, authorising them to make Captures of British Vessels and Cargoes.

In Congress, April 3, 1776.

I.

You may, by Force of Arms, attack, subdue, and take all Ships and other Vessels belonging to the Inhabitants of Great Britain, on the High Seas, or between high water and low water Marks, except Ships and Vessels bringing Persons who intend to settle and reside in the United Colonies, or bringing Arms, Ammunition or

Warlike Stores to the said Colonies, for the use of such Inhabitants thereof as are Friends to the American Cause, which you shall suffer to pass unmolested, the Commanders thereof permitting a peaceable Search, and giving satisfactory information of the contents of the Ladings, and Destinations of the Voyages.

II.

You may, by force of Arms, attack, subdue, and take all Ships and other Vessels whatsoever carrying Soldiers, Arms, Gun powder, Ammunition, Provisions, or any other contraband Goods, to any of the British Armies or Ships of War employed against these Colonies.

III.

You shall bring such Ships and Vessels as you shall take, with their Guns, Rigging, Tackle, Apparel, Furniture and Ladings, to some convenient Port or Ports of the United Colonies, that Proceedings may thereupon be had in due Form before the Courts which are or shall be there appointed to hear and determine Causes civil and maritime.

IV.

You or one of your Chief Officers shall bring or send the Master and Pilot and one or more principal Person or Persons of the Company of every Ship or Vessel by you taken, as soon after the Capture as may be, to the Judge or Judges of such Courts as aforesaid, to be examined upon Oath, and make Answer to the Interrogatories which may be propounded touching the interest or Property of the Ship or Vessel and her Lading; and at the same Time you shall deliver or cause to be delivered to the Judge or Judges, all Passes, Sea Briefs, Charter Parties, Bills of Lading, Cockets, Letters, and other Documents and Writings found on Board, proving the said Papers by the Affidavit of yourself, or of some other Person present at the Capture, to be produced as they were received, without Fraud, Addition, Subduction, or Embezzlement.

V.

You shall keep and preserve every Ship or Vessel and Cargo by you taken, until they shall by Sentence of a Court properly authorised be adjudged lawful Prize, not selling, spoiling, wasting, or diminishing the same or breaking the Bulk thereof, nor suffering any such thing to be done.

VI.

If you, or any of your Officers or Crew shall, in cold Blood, kill or maim, or by Torture or otherwise, cruelly, inhumanly, and contrary to common Usage and the Practice of civilized Nations in War, treat any Person or Persons surprised in the Ship or Vessel you shall take, the Offender shall be severely punished.

VII.

You shall, by all convenient Opportunities, send to Congress written Accounts of the Captures you shall make, with the Number and Names of the Captives, Copies of your journal from Time to Time, and Intelligence of what may occur or be discovered concerning the Designs of the Enemy, and the Destinations, Motions, and Operations of their Fleets and Armies.

VIII.

One Third, at the least, of your whole Company shall be Land Men.

IX.

You shall not ransom any Prisoners or Captives, but shall dispose of them in such Manner as the Congress, or if that be not fitting in the Colony whither they shall be brought, as the General Assembly, Convention, or Council or Committee of Safety of such Colony shall direct.

X.

You shall observe all such further Instructions as Congress shall hereafter give in the Premises, when you shall have Notice thereof.

XI.

If you shall do any Thing contrary to these Instructions, or to others hereafter to be given, or willingly suffer such Thing to be done, you shall not only forfeit your Commission, and be liable to an Action for Breach of the Condition of your Bond, but be responsible to the Party grieved for Damages sustained by such Mal-versation.

By Order of Congress.

John Hancock, President.

Additional Instructions and Letter of Marque and Reprisal.

In Congress, April 3, 1776.

RESOLVED, That every Person intending to set forth and fit out a Private Ship or Vessel of War, and applying for a Commission or Letters of Marque and Reprisal for that Purpose, shall produce a Writing, subscribed by him, containing the Name, and Tonnage or Burthen of the Ship or Vessel, the Number of her Guns, with their Weight of Metal, the Name and Place of Residence of the Owner or Owners, the Names of the Commander and other Officers, the Number of the Crew, and the Quantity of Provisions and Warlike Stores; which Writing shall be delivered to the Secretary of Congress, or to the Clerk of the House of Representatives, Convention or Council or Committee of Safety of the Colony in which the Ship or Vessel shall be, to be transmitted to the said Secretary, and shall be registered by him. And that the Commander of the Ship or Vessel, before the Commission or Letter of Marque and Reprisal may be granted, shall, together with sufficient Sureties, seal and deliver a Bond, in the Penalty of Five Thousand Dollars, if the Vessel be on of One Hundred Tons, or under, or Ten Thousand Dollars, if of greater Burthen, payable to the President of the Congress in Trust for the Use of the United Colonies, with Condition in the Form following, to wit,

"The Condition of this Obligation is Such, That if the abovebounden (name of commander) who is Commander of the (vessel type) called (name of vessel) belonging to (name of owner) of (city) in the Colony of (colony) mounting (quantity) Carriage Guns, and navigated by (quantity) Men, and who hath applied for a Commission or Letters of Marque and Reprisal, to arm, equip and set forth to Sea the said (vessel) as a Private Ship of War, and to make Captures of British Vessels and Cargoes, shall not exceed or transgress the Powers and Authorities which shall be contained in the said Commission, but shall in all Things observe and conduct himself and govern his Crew by and according to the same, and certain Instructions therewith to be delivered, and such other Instructions as may hereafter be given to him; and shall make Reparation for all Damages sustained by any Misconduct or unwarrantable Proceedings of himself, or the Officers or Crew of the said (vessel) Then this Obligation shall be void, or else remain in Force.

Sealed and Delivered in Presence of, (witness)

Which Bond shall be lodged with the said Secretary of Congress.

By Order of Congress,

John Hancock, President.

Privateer Recruiting Advertisement.
Beverly, Massachusetts, 1776.

Now fitting for a Privateer,
In the Harbour of Beverly,
The Brigantine *Washington*,
A Strong, good vessel for that purpose and a prime sailer.
Any Seamen or Landmen that have an inclination to
Make their Fortunes in a few Months,
May have an Opportunity, by applying to
JOHN DYSON.
Beverly, September 17th, 1776.

British Privateer Recruiting Advertisement.
Nova Scotia Gazette, 1779.

All Gentlemen Volunteers:
Seaman, and able bodied Landsman, who wish to acquire
Riches and honor
Are invited to repair on board the
Revenge Privateer ship of War
Now laying in Halifax Harbour
Mounting Thirty Carriage Guns, with Carronades, swivels,
&c. &c. bound on a Cruise to the Southward for four Months
Against the French, and all his Majesty's enemies, and
Then to return to this harbour.
All volunteers will be received on board the said ship - or by
Captain James Gandy
At his Rendezvouse at
Mr. Proud's Tavern near the Chandlery,
Where they will meet with all due Encouragement,
And the best treatment: Proper Advance will be given.

January 12, 1779

Privateer Recruiting Advertisement.
Boston Gazette, 1780.

An Invitation to all brave Seamen and Mariners, who have an inclination to serve their Country and make their Fortunes.

The grand Privateer Ship *DEANE*,

Commanded by Elisha Hinman, Esq., and prov'd to be a very capital Sailor, will sail on a Cruise against the Enemies of the United States of America, by the 20th instant. The *DEANE* mounts thirty Carriage Guns, and is excellently well calculated for Attacks, Defence and Pursuit -- This therefore is to invite all those Jolly Fellows, who love their Country, and want to make their Fortunes at one Stroke, to repair immediately to the Rendezvous at the Head of His Excellency Governor Hancock's Wharf, where they will be received with a hearty Welcome by a Number of Brave Fellows there assembled, and treated with that excellent Liquor call'd GROG which is allow'd by all true Seamen, to be the LIQUOR OF LIFE.

President's Instructions to Private Armed Vessels.[5]
Confederate President's Instructions for Privateers, 1861.

1. The tenor of your commission under the act of Congress, entitled "An act, recognizing the existence of war between the United States and the Confederate States; and concerning letters of marque, prizes, and prize goods," a copy of

5 An Act recognizing the existence of War between the United States and the Confederate States; and concerning letters of marque, prizes, and prize goods.

which is hereto annexed, will be kept constantly in your view. The high seas, referred to in your commissions, you will understand generally, to refer to low water mark; but with the exception of the space within one league, or three miles from the shore of countries at peace both with the United States and the Confederate States. You may nevertheless execute your commission within that distance of the shore of a nation at war with the United States, and even on the water within the jurisdiction of such nation, if permitted to do so.

2. You are to pay the strictest regard to the rights of neutral powers, and the usages of civilized nations; and in all your proceedings towards neutral vessels, you are to give them as little molestation or interruption as will consist with the right of ascertaining their neutral character, and of detaining and bringing them in for regular adjudication in the proper cases.

   You are particularly to avoid even the appearance of using force or seduction, with a view to deprive such vessels of their crews or of their passengers, other than persons in the military service of the enemy.

3. Towards enemy vessels and their crews, you are to proceed in exercising the rights of war, with all the justice and humanity which characterize this Government and its citizens.

4. The master, and one or more of the principal persons belonging to the captured vessels, are to be sent, as soon after the capture as may be, to the judge or judges of the proper court in the Confederate States, to be examined upon oath touching the interest or property of the captured

vessel and her lading; and at the same time, are to be delivered to the judge or judges, all papers, charter parties, bills of lading, letters and other documents, and writings found on board; the said papers to be proved by the affidavit of the commander of the capturing vessels, or some other person present at the capture, to be produced as they were received, without fraud, addition, subduction or embezzlement.

5. Property, even of the enemy, is exempt from seizure on neutral vessels, unless it be contraband of war.

   If goods contraband of war are found on any neutral vessel, and the commander thereof shall offer to deliver them up, the offer shall be accepted, and the vessel left at liberty to pursue its voyage, unless the quantity of contraband goods be greater than can be conveniently received on board your vessel, in which case the neutral vessel may be carried into port for the delivery of the contraband goods.

The following articles are deemed by this Government contraband of war, as well as others that are so declared by the law of nations, viz:

All arms and implements, serving for the purposes of war by land or sea, such as cannons, mortars, guns, muskets, rifles, pistols, petards, bombs, grenades, ball, shot, shell, fuses, pikes, swords, bayonets, javelins, lances, horse furniture, holsters, belts, and generally all other implements of war.

Also, timber for ship building, pitch, tar, rosin, copper in sheets, sails, hemp, cordage, and generally whatever may serve directly to the equipment of vessels, unwrought iron and planks only excepted.

Neutral vessels conveying enemies' despatches or military

persons in the service of the enemy, forfeit their neutral character, and are liable to capture and condemnation. But this rule does not apply to neutral vessels bearing despatches from the public ministers or embassadors of the enemy residing in neutral countries.

By the command of the President of the Confederate States.

Robert Toombs,

Secretary of State.

An Act Regulating the sale of Prizes, and the distribution thereof.[6]

Second session of the provisional Congress of the Confederate States, May 14, 1861.

1. *The Congress of the Confederate States of America do enact,* That all prizes of vessels and property captured by private armed ships, in pursuance of the act passed by Congress recognizing the existence of war between the United States and the Confederate States, and concerning letters of marque, prizes and prize goods, which may be condemned in any court of the Confederate States, shall be sold at public auction by the marshal of the district in which the same shall be condemned, within sixty days after the condemnation thereof—sufficient notice of the time and place and condition of sale being first given—on such day or days, on such terms of credit, and in such lots or proportions as may be designated by the owner or owners, or agent of the owner or owners, of the privateer which may have captured the same: *Provided,* That the term of such credit shall not exceed ninety days. And the said marshal is hereby directed to take

6 Acts and Resolutions of the Second Session of the Provisional Congress of the Confederate States, 1861.

and receive from the purchaser or purchasers of such prize vessel and property, the money therefor, or his, her or their promissory notes, with endorsers, to be approved by the owner or owners of the privateer, to the amount of the purchase, payable according to the terms thereof.

2. That upon all duties, costs and charges being paid according to law, the said marshal shall, on demand, deliver and pay over to the owner or owners of the privateer, or to the agent of such owner or owners of the privateer which may have captured such prize vessel and property, a just and equal proportion of the funds received on account of the sale thereof, and of the promissory notes directed to be taken as aforesaid, to which the said owner or owners may be entitled, according to the articles of agreement between the said owner or owners and the officers and crew of the said privateer; and a just and equal proportion of the proceeds of the sale as aforesaid, shall, on demand, be also paid over by the said marshal to the officers and crew of the said privateer, or to their agent or agents. And if there be no written agreement, it shall be the duty of the marshal to pay over, in manner as aforesaid, one moiety of the proceeds of the sale of such prize vessel and property to the owner or owners of the privateer which may have captured the same, and the other moiety of the said proceeds to the agent or agents of the officers and crew of the said privateer, to be distributed according to law, or to any agreement by them made: *Provided,* The said officers and crew, or their agent or agents, shall have first refunded to the owner or owners, or to the agent of the owner or owners of the privateer aforesaid, the full amount of advances which shall have been

made by the owner or owners of the privateer to the officers and crew thereof.

3. That for the selling prize property and receiving and paying over the proceeds as aforesaid, the marshal shall be entitled to a commission of one per cent, and no more, first deducting all duties, costs and charges which may have accrued on said property: *Provided,* That on no case of condemnation and sale of any one prize vessel and cargo shall the commissions of the marshal exceed two hundred and fifty dollars.

4. That it shall be the duty of the marshal, within fifteen days after any sale of prize property, to file in the office of the clerk of the district court of the district wherein such sale may be made, a just and true account of the sales of such prize property, and of all duties and charges there on, together with a statement thereto annexed of the promissory notes taken on account thereof, which account shall be verified by the oath of the said marshal; and if the said marshal shall wilfully neglect or refuse to file such account, he shall forfeit and pay the sum of five hundred dollars for each omission or refusal as aforesaid, to be recovered in an action of debt by any person interested in such sale, and suing for the said penalty, on account of the party or parties interested in the prize vessel or property sold as aforesaid, in any court having cognizance thereof.

5. That the owner or owners of any private armed vessel or vessels, or their agent or agents, may, at any time before a libel shall be filed against any captured vessel or her cargo, remove the same from any port into which such prize vessel or property may be first brought, to any other port in

the Confederate States, to be designated at the time of the removal as aforesaid, subject to the same restrictions and complying with the same regulations with respect to the payment of duties which are provided by law in relation to other vessels arriving in port with cargoes subject to the payment of duties: *Provided,* That before such removal the said captured property shall not have been attached at the suit of any adverse claimant, or a claim against the same have been interposed in behalf of the Confederate States.

Approved May 14, 1861.

Made in the USA
Las Vegas, NV
14 March 2021

19570258R00135